OVERCOMING TEMPTATION

BRUCE WILKINSON

WITH HEATHER HAIR

HARVEST HOUSE PUBLISHERS
EUGENE, OREGON

Cover by Darren Welch Design

Overcoming Temptation
Copyright © 2018 Bruce Wilkinson
Published by Harvest House Publishers
Eugene, Oregon 97408
www.harvesthousepublishers.com

ISBN 978-0-7369-7183-6 (pbk.)
ISBN 978-0-7369-7184-3 (eBook)

Library of Congress Cataloging-in-Publication Data

Names: Wilkinson, Bruce, author.
Title: Overcoming temptation / Bruce Wilkinson.
Description: Eugene : Harvest House Publishers, 2018.
Identifiers: LCCN 2018009574 (print) | LCCN 2018016704 (ebook) | ISBN 9780736971843 (ebook) | ISBN 9780736971836 (pbk.)
Subjects: LCSH: Temptation. | Prayer—Christianity.
Classification: LCC BT725 (ebook) | LCC BT725 .W44 2018 (print) | DDC 242/.4—dc23
LC record available at https://lccn.loc.gov/2018009574

Printed in the United States of America

18 19 20 21 22 23 24 25 26 / BP-CD / 10 9 8 7 6 5 4 3 2 1

CONTENTS

We…have a High Priest who…

was in all points tempted

as we are, yet without sin.

HEBREWS 4:15

CHAPTER ONE

Temptations Are Your Desires Gone Astray

A wise old preacher was walking through a large shopping mall when one of the young men in his church came up beside him and started talking to him about his struggle with various temptations. The young man said that someday he hoped to live so holy a life that he wouldn't have any more temptations and asked his trusted pastor if he knew the secret to get there.

The old sage smiled and said, "So, do you really want to have a life without temptations? Well, there's only one way any of us can get above temptations, but I'm not sure you're ready for that yet."

The young man stopped walking. "Yes, I do! I'll do anything to get rid of my temptations; they're hounding me!"

"Well," the preacher shrugged and said, "I'm afraid you aren't wealthy enough. You don't live in a big enough house yet."

"What? What do you mean? I need to be wealthy and live in a big house—how big?"

The old man nodded—he was enjoying this little theological conversation. "I guess you could call it one of those big estates or mansions. Maybe even with those tall columns outside and sprawling gardens and fountains."

"But, Pastor, you live in a normal house like we do…so I guess you aren't free of temptations?"

"Nope. Not even close."

"Well, will you ever be free?"

"Absolutely, son, no doubt about it—my long-term plans guarantee that. It's only a matter of time."

"You mean you have some wealthy relative or something?"

"Yup, you hit the nail on the head. And when I get my inheritance, He's promised me a really magnificent place to live too! Only one problem though, son. My relative said I can only get that inheritance when I die, not one day before." By this time, he could see the young man was barely able to cope with what he was saying. "And when I arrive, my temptations will all be gone—every single one of them. I guess you could say I'm dying to get there!

"You see, the only way to get free of all your temptations is to die, go to heaven, and dwell in the mansion Jesus has prepared for all who love Him. Because on this side of eternity, temptations grow like weeds! You'll never be free of them—instead, you need to learn how to overcome them."

Now that's the truth, isn't it? None of us will ever be free of temptations until our life on earth is finally over. Until then, temptations may be the largest threat you face. As we prepare to learn the shocking information that the Bible reveals about temptations, let me ask you a foundational question:

How big of a sin are your temptations?

To answer that important question, you need to understand a few foundational biblical truths about your temptations:

1. Temptations are not sinful or anything you should be ashamed of.

Many people who are reading this book, like you are at this moment, have always felt ashamed of their temptations. Why? Because they have assumed that temptations must be sinful. That's probably the reason no one ever speaks about their temptations—we are ashamed of them.

But what would you do if you discovered that the Bible clearly states that temptations are not a sin? Hebrews 4:15 contains the startling information:

> We do not have a High Priest who cannot sympathize with our weaknesses, but was in all points *tempted as we are, yet without sin.*

Jesus was tempted in all points like we are, but He never sinned! If temptations were a sin, then Jesus sinned, because He was tempted just like we are. But the Bible clearly states that Jesus was sinless (2 Corinthians 5:21; 1 John 3:5). Therefore, temptations cannot be a sin or anything to be ashamed of. The Bible openly states Jesus was tempted in "all" ways "as we are." Temptations are as normal as living and breathing. But as you will soon learn, how you feel about your temptations greatly affects whether they will give birth to sin.

2. Temptations are experienced by every single human being.

No one escapes the onslaught of temptations. Not a single person. Hebrews 4:15 reveals that everyone is tempted: "But was in all points tempted as we are." Did you see the words "as we are," without any exceptions or limitations? You are tempted; she is tempted; he is tempted; they are tempted; I am tempted.

3. Temptations come to everyone, no matter how godly.

Far too many of us are tragically misinformed about the truth of temptations. People assume that the more godly a person becomes, the less temptations that person will face. Yet the most godly of all humans who ever lived, Jesus Christ, was "in all points tempted as we are"! Jesus wasn't just tempted a little, but in "all" ways. Shocking, isn't it? Godliness does not in any way limit the number of temptations we may receive.

In fact, when you read many of the famous Christian classics written by saints from across history, they all lament about the number and strength of their temptations. Over time, however, the nature of their temptations seemed to change from the more serious sins to the far lesser sins. Temptations can be conquered the more that we walk with the Lord, but they remain present in our lives until we cross over to the other side.

> No man knows how bad he is till he has tried very hard to be good. A silly idea is current that good people do not know what temptation means.
>
> —C. S. LEWIS

4. Temptations are normal, God-given desires that seek to trespass God's boundaries.

What exactly are temptations? The answer may surprise you because temptations are based on the normal desires that God gave to all of us but with one thing out of place: Those desires seek to trespass the boundaries God established for us.

In other words, a temptation is simply a good desire gone bad!

Our God-given desires become temptations when we desire too much, or go too far, or seek to fulfill them in the wrong place or with the wrong person. Temptations are simply the inner push of our normal desires to overstep God's boundaries. Often the Bible calls our sins a trespass, which means to go beyond a clear boundary into forbidden or off-limits territory.

Every single temptation is rooted in a normal desire. God Himself gave us our desires and wants us to learn through experience to honor and obey His stated boundaries.

Take the normal desire to eat, for instance. God created food for mankind to sustain us and for us to enjoy. We feel hunger as a result of our God-given desire to eat. When, then, does our desire to eat become a temptation? When we succumb to the desire to eat too much and move into the sin of gluttony. Temptation is simply the desire to eat pushed too far, beyond the boundaries of self-control that God wants us to have.

THE GREAT SECRET OF
**OVERCOMING SIN
IN YOUR LIFE**
IS TO FOCUS ON DEFEATING THE
TEMPTATIONS YOU FACE,
AND NOT SO MUCH
ON DEFEATING THE SINS
THAT ARE THE RESULT
OF YOUR CHOICE TO GIVE IN TO
YOUR TEMPTATIONS.

The New Testament word *desire* is translated from the Greek verb *epithymeo.* This Greek word is translated "desire" eight times, "covet" three times, "lust" three times, and "lust after" one time. How then do we know what to translate the single Greek word—"desire" or "lust"? Take a look at the following two verses that use the word *eipthymeo* but in very different ways, one translated as "desire" and the other as "lust."

> This is a faithful saying: If a man *desires* the position of a bishop, he desires a good work (1 Timothy 3:1).

> I say to you that whoever looks at a woman to *lust* for her has already committed adultery with her in his heart (Matthew 5:28).

The translators knew that the root *epithymeo* means "to desire" in normal usage (desiring to be a bishop is a good thing), but when that desire focused on an unhealthy or sinful object, they translated it with the word "lust." Lust is simply strong desire, but when that strong desire is for an inappropriate action such as adultery, then *epithymeo* is better translated "lust."

The same word, *epithymeo*, is also translated in the King James to the word "covet," even though the word still means desire. For instance, Paul wrote in Acts 20:33: "I have *coveted* no one's silver or gold or apparel." Why does the Bible translate "desire" as "covet"? Simply because Paul was discussing a lack of desire for property that didn't belong to him.

These illustrations all prove the point that temptations

are simply normal desires that entice us to go beyond the boundaries God has established for all of us. Every single temptation you will ever experience is based upon normal desires. When you don't allow your desires to go too far or too fast, you don't sin. Since temptations are simply God-given desires, they aren't sinful but are normal. What you and I do with our desires, however, determines if we walk in obedience or stray into disobedience.

5. Temptations precede every single sin; if you overcome temptations, you won't sin.

Now you are prepared to learn a profound truth that will help you immensely in your Christian walk: Every sin you have ever committed or will commit is always—and I mean always—preceded by a temptation! If you aren't tempted, guess what? You won't sin!

You must embrace this all-important fact: Temptations precede every sin.

With that in mind, look at how Hebrews 4:15 connects temptations and sin: "But was in all points *tempted* as we are, yet *without sin.*"

Jesus was tempted, but He did not permit the desires He felt to find inappropriate fulfilment in any selfish or sinful act. This means Jesus felt the desire, just like all of us do; He just chose not to allow those desires to give birth to sin.

Could it be, therefore, that the great overlooked secret of overcoming sin in your life is to focus on defeating the temptations you face, and not so much on defeating the sins that are the result of your choice to give in to your temptations! Here are the three stages working in every temptation:

Desire → Temptation → Sin

If you tone down the intensity of your wrongful desire, then temptations flee into the darkness, powerless and defeated. When you defeat a temptation, you no longer have to struggle with that particular desire to sin because you exercised your self-discipline and said no to that straying desire.

These opening chapters lay the solid foundation for the second half of the book, where you are led through a biblical process of praying to find victory over specific temptations. But first we are going to unmask your temptations—so hold on, as there are some shocking revelations on the way that will greatly empower you to defeat your temptations!

No temptation has overtaken you

except such as is common to man;

but God is faithful, who will not allow

you to be tempted beyond what you are able,

but with the temptation will also

make the way of escape,

that you may be able to bear it.

1 CORINTHIANS 10:13

CHAPTER TWO

The Seven Revelations About Your Temptations

One of the most frequently quoted passages in the Bible is found in Hosea 4:6: "My people are destroyed for lack of knowledge." God was lamenting that His people were destroyed because of the absence of something, because of their "lack of knowledge." Whenever the truth of Scriptures is missing in any given area, the results are always the same: Sin runs rampant. Whenever a massive amount of truth is absent, then the culture and nation inevitably spiral out of control.

This book is a purposeful step in reversing this negative downward trend so that the opposite could be true: "My people are flourishing for an abundance of My truth!" The truths in these opening chapters are powerfully transforming. The further you progress through these pages, the more truth will come rushing into your heart, and if you choose to apply that truth, it will transform your life. No matter what condition you feel your life may be in at this moment, if you apply these powerful secrets in your life, you will experience the opposite of destruction!

Unfortunately, we may have all heard far too much preaching and teaching on sin and not nearly enough on our temptations to sin. If you're like the average person, you may never have heard a sermon explaining what the Bible teaches about our temptations. Thankfully, in 1 Corinthians 10:13 we find a summary of seven important revelations about everyone's temptations:

> No temptation has overtaken you except such as is common to man; but God is faithful, who will not allow you to be tempted beyond what you are able, but with the temptation will also make the way of escape, that you may be able to bear it.

Let's take a look at each of the seven facts revealed about your temptations, one at a time.

1. Temptations are not passive but are active and seek to seize and overtake you.

"No temptation *has overtaken you*."

When you read this verse carefully, you will discover that it discusses temptations in your past, in your present, and finally, in your future. The words "has overtaken you" focuses on your past experiences with temptations. Paul, the author of 1 Corinthians, wants us to know that every single temptation you have ever faced has achieved something very specific: The temptation has "overtaken you."

Temptations are not neutral or passive; they are active. Note the verse states that a temptation overtakes you. *To overtake* means "to catch up with" in traveling or pursuing, like a car on the freeway overtakes and passes you. Never forget that your temptations are after you on the freeway of life. Get off at the next exit and leave them behind!

"Overtake" is translated from the Greek word *lambano*, which simply means "to take, to lay hold of." You are not seeking to overtake yourself, but temptations are. Never forget this major difference:

> Temptations are seeking to overtake you.
> You are not seeking to tempt yourself.

Lambano is also translated as "take" and is used to describe what occurred in the Upper Room at the Last Supper. Matthew 26:26 uses the term twice: "As they were eating, Jesus *took* bread, blessed and broke it, and gave it to the disciples and said, '*Take*, eat; this is My body.'" Jesus reached over and took up the bread and then told the disciples to take it as well. In this case, Jesus did the action of taking ahold of the bread, whereas in our passage, temptation takes ahold of "you."

This clarifies everyone's experience when, seemingly out of the blue, you see something or think something and suddenly you feel a strong temptation to sin. Until that moment, you had no thought of sinning—the temptation actively overtook you until you felt a desire that wasn't of your own planning or intention.

In your mind you must separate two very different elements: you and your temptations. Why? Because you are not your temptations; rather, you experience temptations. Temptations seek to overtake you. You are not equal to your temptations; they are powerful, and their intent is to overwhelm you. In your mind, then, never misunderstand this fact: Temptations are not your friends. They aren't passive. They aren't neutral. They have a specific goal in mind: to entice you to sin.

> Temptation: The fiend at my elbow.
> **—WILLIAM SHAKESPEARE**

Temptations actively pursue you with a very specific goal in mind: to arouse your desire for something or someone that God has ordained to be off-limits for you. In the next chapter you are going to learn the seven stages every single temptation uses to trap you. But for now, realize temptations are after you!

2. Temptations are never unique just to you but are common to everyone.

"No temptation has overtaken you *except such as is common to man.*"

After one men's meeting when I was speaking about personal holiness, especially in sexual areas, a young man approached me, obviously under conviction. He whispered that he desperately needed to break free from his immoral lifestyle but just couldn't. He shared that he was living with a woman at the present and had slept around with others. I asked him why he didn't choose to stop his sexual immorality, and he said he wished he could but he just felt powerless in the face of his overwhelming sexual temptations.

I nodded my head and smiled. "Your sex drive must be really strong."

His face lit up. "Well, I'm glad you understand. My sex drive is so unbelievably strong that my temptations overpower me."

I nodded again. "Your sex drive is probably many times stronger than the normal man's, isn't it?"

He blushed sheepishly and nodded in quick agreement. Finally, it appeared, he had found someone who understood: His sin wasn't really his fault—it was those giant, overpowering temptations that were unique to him.

I asked him if it would make any difference to him if those giant, massive temptations were brought down to normal size, like those a normal man might face.

"Wow!" he exclaimed. "I'd give anything to have normal temptations. Why, I'd finally be able to say no and stop."

Then I turned and scanned the audience. "So, if your temptations were the more common size, like Chuck's or Bob's or Forest's, what would you do?"

He brightened and replied, "Well, I'd move out of my girlfriend's house today and stop being immoral." It was obvious that he believed no one could fix his problem—he was trapped, without hope. It wasn't really his problem because God unfortunately had given him such a powerful sex drive.

So I turned in my Bible to this verse, 1 Corinthians 10:13, and had him read it out loud. When he came to this phrase, "No temptation has overtaken you except such as is *common to man*," he almost choked on the words. I quietly said,

NEVER AGAIN BUY INTO ONE OF
THE UNIVERSAL TRAPS SET BY THE
TEMPTATION HORDE;

**YOUR TEMPTATIONS
ARE NOT UNIQUE**

BUT ARE JUST LIKE EVERYONE
ELSE'S IN THE WORLD.

"Your temptations are not unusual or stronger than anyone else's—they are the garden-variety temptations present in every man's life."

He had bought into the lie that his temptations were not common but were unique, far larger than anyone else's. But the Bible revealed they weren't. I pointed to some of my friends who had shared some of their sexual temptations with me and said, "Each man has the same temptations as you do—only they said no and you said yes."

This story provides a clear explanation of why we have a chapter just focused on the truth about our temptations—because all of us can become self-deceived about our temptations and believe that they are so powerful that we can't help but sin. But never forget, the Bible clearly states that your temptations are the same as everyone else's!

First Corinthians 10:13 says that every one of our temptations are experienced by every other member of the human race. The Greek word *anthropinos* simply means "after the manner of mankind" or "of human nature." James 3:7 uses the same word: "For every kind of beast and bird, of reptile and creature of the sea, is tamed and has been tamed by *mankind*." This truth is further underscored by Hebrews 4:15: "For we do not have a High Priest who cannot sympathize with our weaknesses, but *was in all points tempted as we are*, yet without sin." Because Jesus was fully a man, He experienced the same temptations that all people face.

Therefore, never again buy into one of the universal traps set by the temptation horde; your temptations are not unique but are just like everyone else's in the world. However, you can weaken your resolve by repeatedly choosing to sin in any given area—but the basic temptation is the same as everyone else's.

3. Temptations overtake you, but during the entire process, God remains faithful.

> "No temptation has overtaken you except such as is common to man; *but God is faithful.*"

At this point, the verse transitions from your past to the present, from "has overtaken" to "God is faithful."

First Corinthians 10:13 lies in the middle of a chapter that outlines many of the tragic sins of Israel during their 40 years of wilderness wandering, including idolatry, widespread sexual immorality, testing God, and "lusting after evil things." Then right in the middle of this passage you'll find something you never would have expected. A third entity is introduced. First your temptations, then you, and now God.

Temptations have overtaken all of us, "but God." Who would have expected God would be involved in this chapter on temptations and sin and failure? But God did what? Before explaining this "but God," I would like to underscore one major point a bit more.

Earlier I emphasized that temptations are not a sin in any way because Jesus Himself was tempted in all ways but without sin. It's not until you are fully free from the false guilt about being tempted—not just tempted for "little" sins, but even for very serious ones like adultery, murder, and idolatry—that you can be fully released to understand and walk in this next set of truths. Temptations, no matter what sin you are tempted to commit, are never, ever a sin! They aren't half sins. They aren't sinful a little bit. No sin resides in temptations. Temptations seek to lure us to sin, but they are not sin itself. Separate completely two related but independent ideas: Temptations are not sins. Temptations are not sinful. Temptations are not you.

Therefore, you should have absolutely no guilt about being tempted.

Being tempted isn't anything to feel shame or self-hatred over. Temptations are simply God-given desires that seek to push you beyond the line God has drawn in the sand: "You may walk up to this line, but do not go beyond it." That's what the word *transgress* means, to go beyond an established standard.

It's only when you accept this powerful biblical truth that you will be free to approach God, realizing that He is not upset that you are being tempted! Remember, He sees temptations as a normal plight of mankind.

Let me prove that to you. Think about Adam and Eve in the Garden of Eden. Satan tempted Eve *before* Adam or Eve had sinned. She didn't sin when she wrestled with the temptation; she sinned when she willfully chose to embrace the temptation and take the forbidden fruit. She was tempted before there was sin!

Whenever we aren't sinning, we aren't sinning. Experiencing a temptation is never a sin. In fact, if you choose not to submit to your temptation, you are pleasing the Lord. While you were feeling temptation, you weren't displeasing God! While you struggled deeply with a given temptation, every moment of that struggle was not displeasing to God! The struggle with temptation isn't a sin.

In fact, as shocking as it may seem, you'll soon discover that God Himself is very involved in the process of your temptation. But James 1:13 makes it clear beyond any question that God is never the *cause* of any of your temptations:

"Let no one say when he is tempted, 'I am tempted by God'; for God cannot be tempted by evil, nor does He Himself tempt anyone."

"But God" is in direct contrast to "temptations overtake you." "Temptations overtake you" is in direct opposition to "But God"! The temptations seek your sin, while God seeks your victory over temptation.

Even your most powerful temptations are no match for your all-powerful God.

"But God" is…what? What characteristic does God want us to remember about Him when we are faced with our irritating and unwanted temptations? Think about it: Who wakes up in the morning hoping, *Today I hope to be strongly tempted for all kinds of sins*?

The Corinthians verse continues with, "But God is faithful," and then gives the unexpected and stunning reasons that prove God's enduring faithfulness to us.

Faithful means "to be loyal, true to one's word and promises, steady in allegiance or affection, thorough in the performance of duty." Why is God's faithfulness brought into the topic of our temptations? Because God commanded us in 1 Peter 1:15-16, "As He who called you is holy, you also be holy in *all your conduct*, because it is written, 'Be holy, for I am holy.'" The greatest hindrance to our holiness is our sin; the precursor to every one of our sins is nothing less than our temptations.

No temptation, no sin; temptation creates the desire to sin.

Think about it: What happens if our temptations are too overpowering? Or if we are too weak one day for one reason or another? Or if we try with all our heart but cannot find a way not to sin? Or what happens if our temptations never stop in one area, for minutes, hours, or days on end, and we just can't bear it any longer?

What kind of God would we have if on one hand He commands us to be "holy" and then on the other hand allows temptations to overpower us? But God is faithful, right in the middle of our temptations. That's why you must accept that your temptations are not sinful but are normal.

As you will soon see, the Bible teaches that God's faithfulness to us causes Him to intervene on our behalf when we are tempted. As 2 Peter 2:9 states, "The Lord knows how to deliver the godly *out of temptations*." At this point, you may be wondering, *Well, okay, but how does God deliver me out of my temptations?*

Now it's time to see how God's faithfulness works on our behalf in every temptation we may face.

4. Temptations are always limited in their power by God Himself.

"God is faithful, *who will not allow you to be tempted beyond* what you are able."

This passage is unique as it reveals one major area where God will not permit something to occur in your life. He limits the power of every temptation that you have faced, are facing, or will ever face: God "*will not allow you to be tempted beyond* what you are able"!

The strength of our temptations is always governed by the Almighty: "This temptation can go this far, but no further." Temptations always seek to push us beyond God's standards; God always limits the amount of "push" in every temptation we will ever face.

The verb phrase "will not allow" is in the future active form, which proves that God Himself actively limits every one of your temptations. The verse doesn't say you won't experience any temptation too strong for you, but rather that God will not permit or allow any overpowering temptations.

 Many years ago, when Darlene and I moved from New Jersey to Dallas, Texas to attend graduate school, we rented a truck to move our belongings 1,600 miles (2,580 kilometers). On the second day, we were ready for the trip to end, and I started pushing the truck to go faster on the seemingly unending freeway. But when the truck hit the speed limit, it would not allow me to go any faster, not even just a few miles per hour more. When we stopped to buy some gas, I asked the mechanic to look at the truck and see if something was wrong. He queried me as to what seemed to be the problem and then started laughing. He smiled and said, "The rental agency put limiters or governors on all their trucks to stop everyone from going even one mile over the speed limit!"

The point? God installed His "Temptation Governor" to limit the power of every single temptation you will ever face. Never again permit yourself to say, "I just couldn't help myself, the temptation was just too strong" because then you would be calling God a liar. But God not only never lies, but He always remains faithful to you.

Years ago, Darlene and I took a long walk in the nearby

woods and I tried to explain the essence of this truth. I said that unless God limited the strength of our temptations, some of them could overwhelm us no matter how much we tried not to give in.

If that wasn't true, then why would God need to limit the strength of our temptations?

At that moment we walked past a massive, magnificent tree standing in the woods. I commented, "That tree has withstood fierce storms over the decades yet stood strong through it all. But a storm could come that was so powerful that even that massive tree would fall. In this illustration, we are the tree, and God promises that He will not allow any storm to be so strong that we had no choice but to fall."

One of the more technical theological concepts is called the "permissive will of God," and it refers to situations that God allows but does not direct. God demonstrated the limits of His permissive will in His debate with Satan over Job. Listen to how God expressed His limits as to how far Satan would be permitted to afflict and tempt Job: "The LORD said to Satan, 'Behold, all that he has is in your power; *only do not lay a hand on his person*'" (Job 1:12). God permitted Satan to attack everything Job had, but he wasn't permitted to "lay a hand on his person." Satan could not go beyond the limitations God established. Neither can our temptations.

Before going any further, reflect on this amazing truth—that God sovereignly and always limits every temptation in your life to never go "beyond what you are able." If you ever looked for a proof of God's personal involvement in your life, this is a clear demonstration, isn't it? God cares so much for you and for your victory over your temptations that He personally limits every temptation so you can definitely overcome them. Therefore, never doubt again or allow yourself to say or think, *But this temptation is just too strong for me.* Instead, just get off that freeway!

While this act of God's faithfulness during our temptations appears to be totally sufficient, God goes even further in serving and protecting you. Wait until you read the next principle.

5. God limits the power of your temptations according to your present ability.

> "God is faithful, who will not allow you to be tempted *beyond what you are able.*"

This verse starts in the past, comments about the present, and completes in the future. In the past, "no temptation has overtaken you except such as is common to man"—so never think what happened in your past was not like what happens to everyone else. In the present that is ever with us, "God is faithful." Last, in the future, God "will not allow you to be tempted beyond what you are able."

Any temptation that will seek to overtake you in the future will be pushed back and limited by God. Just for you.

To me, this truth reflects the most personal of all of God's faithful acts toward us and the various temptations we will experience in our future. Unlike our moving truck that had a standard "governor" that was the same for everyone, God doesn't simply establish a standard limit for each type of temptation. For instance, God doesn't set the "limit" for the strength of temptations for lying for everyone at the 52 level on a scale of 1 to 100, or the temptation of pornography at the 73 level, or the temptation to steal at the 34 level.

Why not? Because all of us are so very different. Some of us never struggle much with the temptation to lie but struggle with stealing on our taxes, and vice versa. Now you can see more clearly the rest of the verse, "beyond what we are able." We all have different "thresholds of temptability" for our various temptations.

How then does God set His Divine Temptation Limiter? Instead of setting standard limits on all the various temptations, He sets limits on temptations one at a time for each individual. For instance, your brother may deeply struggle with the temptation of sexual immorality while you might not struggle with that temptation at all. Maybe you struggle with an addiction to pain medicine from last year's operation, while your brother never even notices when the pain meds are on the counter.

You might have expected the Bible to state, "God is faithful and will not allow you to be tempted beyond what is fair" or "what the average person can handle easily," but He doesn't. God moves from the general topic of temptations and immediately makes it personal, just to you, with the words, "who will not allow you to be tempted *beyond what you are able.*"

God limits each temptation that comes to you in proportion to your ability to stand firm against it at that moment in your life. If you are particularly weak in an area, God may set the limit at 35 while your best friend may be really strong in the same area and can overcome that same temptation at 92.

The word "beyond" is translated from the Greek word *hyper*, which in this passage means "above, beyond, and more than." Remember that line in the sand we discussed previously, the line that the Lord stands in front of and denies your temptation the freedom to go "beyond" that point? "Absolutely not, no further, even by just an inch!"

So how does God determine where that line, your "Temptation Threshold," lies? Is it the seriousness of the potential sin? No. Is it the time of day? No. Is it your age? No. Your educational level? No. Your financial condition at the time? No.

Well then, how does God decide where to draw that line? You are now prepared for the amazing answer: You are the answer. But what about you? The verse lays it out in such clarity there's no room for confusion or uncertainty. The strength of the temptation is based not just on you, but on your ability to fight that temptation at that very moment! "Who will not allow you to be tempted *beyond what you are able*."

The words "beyond what you are able" are translated from the Greek word *dynamai*, which means "to have the ability or power to do something by the virtue of one's own ability and resources, or through a state of mind." In other words, the limit that God sets on the strength of your temptations is determined solely on the basis of the level of your ability at the time to handle that temptation. If your internal strength is low, then God sets the temptation strength at a lower level, but if your internal strength is strong, then so may the temptation be more difficult.

How incredibly kind and gracious of God to take into account where you are in your life at the time of your temptation! Why would God do that for you personally? Because He is faithful and loyal to you and does not want you to be pushed unfairly into sin.

Will you embrace this biblical truth? Never again allow yourself to believe "but the temptation was just too strong for me." It wasn't, even when you were in a most vulnerable state. And it never will be. You can state that confidently because the verb "are able" is in the present tense. In other words, your ability to resist when you are tempted—at that exact moment—will determine the limits God sets on that temptation. He never is the cause, but He certainly is our Divine Governor!

David understood the intricate knowledge that our Heavenly Father has about every part of our life at all times (which is the basis of His knowing the current level of our ability to fight a given temptation) when he wrote in Psalm 139:1-6:

> O LORD, you have examined my heart
>   and know everything about me.
> You know when I sit down or stand up.
>   You know my thoughts even when I'm far away.
> You see me when I travel
>   and when I rest at home.
>   You know everything I do.
> You know what I am going to say
>   even before I say it, LORD.
> You go before me and follow me.
>   You place your hand of blessing on my head.
> Such knowledge is too wonderful for me,
>   too great for me to understand! (NLT).

This principle is one of the most surprising, isn't it? To discover that not only is God not upset or angry or frustrated with any of our temptations—because they aren't wrong but are normal—but instead is personally involved in them. Why? Because He is faithful, and since He commands us to live holy lives and not give in to temptations, He is highly motivated that we succeed. God is not just a little interested in our holiness, my friend; He is vitally committed to us and will not allow us to be tempted "beyond what we are able"!

So, if you are weak today and a temptation creeps up on you, you can be sure that God has pushed down the power of your temptation so you can succeed. His hope? That you will choose not to succumb to your pursuing enemy.

I don't know what you are thinking at this moment, but you may be a bit overwhelmed at the degree of God Almighty's involvement in your temptations. But the verse goes on, revealing an even more shocking revelation of God's protection in every one of our temptations.

God not only limits according to your strength when the temptation comes, but God Himself makes something to help you deal with that temptation that did not exist until the temptation began—and He makes it just for you.

6. Temptations always are accompanied by God's "made way of escape."

"...but *with the temptation will also make the way of escape.*"

Not only is your Father faithful to you at all times, not only will your God limit the strength of each of our temptations at all times, but God goes way beyond what anyone could ever expect: God also "will make the way of escape" from each temptation you face!

God provides a handcrafted path out of each of your temptations.

Did you see the word "also" in this verse, pointing out that whatever occurred before, God acts a third time on your behalf? The first act of God to ensure you won't be overcome is to limit the power of your temptation; the second act of God is to limit the temptation on the basis of your ability to cope at the time; but the third act of God is to provide something that didn't exist until that moment: His specific, hand-tailored, created way of escape.

This verse overflows with truth, doesn't it? This section has three parts: "with the temptation," then "will also make," and finally "the way of escape." When God knows that a temptation is heading toward you, He then acts "with the temptation" (at the same time as) and sovereignly intervenes on your behalf.

The words "will also make" demonstrate that this occurs with the temptation that approaches you—not before the temptation and certainly not after the temptation.

God makes something? Yes. Absolutely. The verb "will make" is in the future active, which means that God is the one who does the "making" when you are tempted in the future. The word "make" comes from the Greek word *poieo*, which means "to be the author of, to be the cause of something, to make ready, to prepare."

When the temptation heads your way, God actively gets involved by preparing the way out of that temptation.

Because the verb is future active, it communicates that this "making" isn't preexisting but is prepared at that specific time of your temptation for your deliverance.

Second Peter 2:9 directly states that God "knows how" to deliver the godly out of temptations: "The Lord knows how to deliver the godly out of temptations." Now you know the method by which God delivers the godly out of temptations—He limits the power of the temptation and makes the way of escape.

The Greek word translated as the "way of escape" comes from *ekbasis*, which is a compound word from *baino*, which means "to go," and *ek*, which means "out of." Greek dictionaries define *ekbasis* as "an egress, a way out, an exit."

Just to ensure we don't misinterpret this concept, the Bible states that God makes "the" way out, not "a" way out. By including the definite article *the*, the Bible makes it clear that God makes a specific and handcrafted exit from each of your temptations. Never again doubt whether you can succeed against any temptation that comes your way!

You don't have to overcome your temptation; you just need to escape it. Like we discussed earlier, if a temptation is seeking to overtake you on the freeway, just take the next exit.

This verse also makes it clear that God doesn't make a few ways out of your temptation; He only makes "*the* way of escape." With each temptation you face, God makes the way out of it, with your name on the exit door.

Recognize that God doesn't make the way to overcome. He makes the way of escape. Escaping the temptation means you overcame it! Only a fool will stay in the fight when the exit door stands wide open. Never believe that the wise or godly thing to do with a temptation is to continue under its clutches; instead, run away through the way of escape that God unlocked for you.

7. Temptations are limited by God and He gives a way of escape so that you can successfully bear them.

"God is faithful, who will not allow you to be tempted beyond what you are able, but with the temptation will also make the way of escape, *that you may be able to bear it.*"

I picture God reaching down with one hand, pushing down the power of my temptations, and with the other hand, carving out a deliverance path out of my temptation. Why does God take such personal interest in our temptations? Because temptations are the only door to our sins. If we do not succumb to our temptations, we will not sin. Sin only occurs when any of us give in to our temptations.

The final part of this verse reveals the reason why God intervenes every time we are tempted.

God deeply desires that we escape each temptation until it ends in defeat and we walk away in victory. The words "you may be able" are in the present tense, which means while you are struggling against the temptation, you will have the freedom to take the way of escape.

The words "to bear" comes from the verb *hypophero*, which means "to bear up under something, to bear patiently and endure until it is completed." It carries the idea that a person continues bearing or enduring something until that situation has ended. In this case, until you take the way of escape.

He doesn't want us to spend 2 minutes and 37 seconds fighting our temptation and then fail. Instead, His intervention is for our complete victory. The temptation ends when it loses all its power because we choose to use God's way of escape.

The Bible never states that God cancels our temptations, but He does provide everything necessary to defeat every single one of our temptations. The deeper you believe these seven revealed facts about your temptations, the more you will walk away from your temptations in total victory.

Temptations are limited; you are able; you can take His way of escape.

In the next chapter you will learn even more profound truth about your temptations because we are going to reveal exactly how every temptation works on you from the first stage to the seventh stage. You'll be able to know what stage you are in at any time and what will come next in your temptation. With that revelation in mind, you'll find it much easier to defeat your next temptation!

Do not let sin reign

in your mortal body,

that you should obey it in its lusts…

Just as you presented your members

as slaves of uncleanness…

so now present your members

as slaves of righteousness for holiness.

ROMANS 6:12,19

CHAPTER THREE

The Seven Stages of Every Temptation

We are now going to enter the Temptation Headquarters and drag their war plans into the broad daylight and make them public for everyone to see and understand. It's finally time to unmask your temptations.

Once you understand what their inner workings are, including each of the seven stages that every temptation uses on you, you will find temptations are far easier to defeat than you ever imagined.

If you don't know how your temptation enemy attacks you, then you are far more likely to be taken advantage of. In the last chapter we discussed how God protects you during your temptations, and in this chapter we will look at the exact opposite: how your temptations attack you. In the final chapter we'll share with you the Seven Tools to Defeat Your Temptations.

Never lose sight of this fact, however: Your temptations aren't your friends; they seek your failure and want you to fall into sin. But at the same time, temptations can be defeated time after time, and during the process your character and conduct will be transformed. What temptations meant for evil, God will use for your good!

Remember, also, that you can defeat any given temptation so often and so thoroughly that it will never bother you again. Why? Because Temptation Headquarters knows you just won't give in to that area, so why bother?

Temptations are aware and cunning. Temptations are deceitful. Temptations are your enemy. Run! The more you run out the way of escape, the more often you will escape.

In this chapter, you are going to understand the precise strategy of temptations because we are going to take a careful look at each of the seven stages that temptations use to overcome you.

So let's jump right into the passage revealing the Seven Stages of Every Temptation!

> Each one is tempted when he is drawn away by his own desires and enticed. Then, when desire has conceived, it gives birth to sin; and sin, when it is full-grown, brings forth death. Do not be deceived, my beloved brethren (James 1:14-16).

There it is in black and white—the inner workings of every temptation. From one stage to the next. All seven stages right in plain view. Each of these stages builds on the previous one, seeks to entice you to commit a particular sin, and then continues to tempt you in that area until that sin rules that part of your life.

It's time for you to learn the actual steps every temptation takes to undo you. No longer will temptations ever be confusing to you. The further you read in this chapter, the more aware you will become of what's been going on in your life without you even being aware of it. Until today.

This type of revelation is often called an awakening or an enlightening. The light will go on as you grasp what's been going on in your temptations but without your conscious awareness. You'll be shocked how temptation has sabotaged you without you knowing it, time after time, right in broad daylight!

So how does every temptation actually begin?

Stage #1: Temptations start when you are distracted and drawn away.

"Each one is tempted *when he is drawn away*."

The opening nine words lay out the launching point of every temptation: "But each one is tempted *when*" something specific happens—when you are "drawn away." Therefore, temptations never begin before this "drawing away" happens to you. You cannot and will not be tempted unless you are pulled "away" from whatever you are doing or thinking to a different focus.

Unless the temptation pulled you away to something, you would not have been able to be tempted. This isn't for some people but every person: "But *each one [every person] is tempted*" only when they have been "drawn away."

"Tempted" is from the Greek word *peirazo*, which is translated in the New Testament as "tempt" 29 times and in the noun form as "tempter" 2 times and means "to try or test one's faith, virtue, or character by enticement to sin." The same word is used referring to Christ's temptation in the wilderness by Satan in Matthew 4:1: "Then Jesus was led up by the Spirit into the wilderness to be *tempted* by the devil."

The verb "tempted" is in the present passive, which means you are the recipient of temptation, not the cause of the temptation.

Although you might think that you cause your own temptations, the Bible states the exact opposite. You don't draw yourself away; temptations do. You receive; you are the passive recipient of the temptation.

Temptations come to you. The temptation takes a specific plan of attack against you. Even when you think that you have purposefully planned on heading to sin, that initial desire was caused by a temptation that drew you away to that thought!

The biblical author uses a series of words in these verses that are also used to describe the process of a fisherman catching a fish, so we are going to use that analogy throughout the chapter.

Picture a beautiful river peacefully meandering through the countryside. On the riverside, a large tree branch overhangs the water shadowing a slow-moving pool of water, right where fish like to gather.

Look through the water and you'll find our unsuspecting school of fish calmly resting, totally unaware that a fisherman has just crept up quietly and is standing out of sight behind the tree. They are all facing upstream so they can swim just a little and rest in this safe location.

Without their awareness, the fisherman quietly prepares his fly rod with the perfect fly as bait for this type of rainbow trout. The fish obviously have no idea what's happening behind the tree.

The crafty fisherman begins swinging that fly with its hidden hook over the water so it looks just like a wandering fly. Then the fisherman carefully lays that fly down so it just touches the water right in front of the fish and then flicks it back up into the air. The moment that fly hits the water, guess what every fish in that pool does? They instantly glance up to see if a delicious bug or fly has fallen off the tree branch into the water.

At that moment, our fisherman knows his secret battle has begun! He knows that at least one fish has been distracted and drawn away, hoping his breakfast bug will return. Now the unsuspecting and innocent fish is thinking about something he wasn't paying attention to until that very moment.

Such is the precise nature of being "drawn away." Temptations occur only when the drawing away has successfully occurred.

Who then distracted the fish? The fisherman, of course. That's exactly how every single temptation starts in everyone's life. All of a sudden you see a person or thing and you are drawn away to look at it. Or a stray thought flashes across your mind, totally off the topic you were considering.

To be effective, the process of being drawn away must

be very subtle and just below the consciousness of the fish. Why? To hide the fact that a fisherman is behind the bait hitting the water. If he mistakenly splashed the water too hard, the fish would instantly know that wasn't a fly.

Similarly, if you are drawn away too abruptly, your innate senses would be alerted and you would be on guard because you knew instinctively that something unusual was going on. Subtle. Delicate. A whisper. A glimpse. A touch.

Sometimes a person can be the source of your being drawn away. Sometimes a wicked entity such as Satan can even be involved. Watch how the first temptation in human history began in Genesis 3:1:

> Now the serpent was more cunning than any beast of the field which the LORD God had made. And he said to the woman, "Has God indeed said, 'You shall not eat of every tree of the garden'?"

The Hebrew word for "cunning" means "to be subtle, shrewd, crafty, and sly." Satan's question was so subtle that Eve thought the serpent only needed some clarification and certainly was not going to attack and lead her to directly disobey God. The moment she heard his question, Eve was drawn away.

Like Eve, we are drawn away from our current thoughts by a subtle distraction. It's subtle because the temptation knows that if you recognize that this is the first step in a whole series of steps to eventually hook you, you would never even pay attention to it but would swim in the opposite direction.

To be "drawn away" means that you were beckoned to leave one area and go to another area.

We don't live our lives in a continuing stage of temptation, do we? Instead, all of us are busy with our families, work, ministry, and friends—and then something happens, and without us being aware of it, we are subtly wooed into thinking or imagining a different area where our temptations are seeking to lure us.

Think of this first stage as a subtle distraction. *Subtle* means "faint," "delicate," and even "difficult to perceive." *Distraction* means "to divide the attention and prevent concentration." It's a diversion, an interruption—but it's hardly noticed.

So what happens next? What do you think every temptation will do next in Stage #2?

Stage #2: Temptations can only tempt because of your inner desire.

"Each one is tempted when he is drawn away *by his own desires.*"

Think about this second stage for a moment: Just because you are drawn away, it doesn't mean that you are feeling anything remotely like a temptation yet. Until you start desiring what you were distracted to, temptation cannot interest you in "biting the bait."

What happens to our unsuspecting fish? The fisherman snaps his line very carefully and allows that handpicked bait—that fly—to hit the water a second time, just a split second longer. It's at that moment that our fish begins to imagine how good that fly would taste as his early-morning snack.

The fisherman knows that until the fish wants the bait, he'll never catch that fish.

It's in that split second when the fish starts to desire the bait that the temptation has begun in earnest. Although fish can't lick their lips with desire, that's exactly what happens.

You see, every temptation must awaken our desire or we'll never consider chasing the bait.

Obviously the fisherman doesn't desire the fly, and the fly doesn't desire the fly—it's only the fish that desires the fly.

Every one of our temptations can only tempt us because it stimulates our personal desire. In this context, it is the desire for something forbidden—tempting us to sin.

When we are drawn away, our attention is pulled away to something. When our desires are stimulated, then the temptation has something to work with inside of us. Think about it: If you aren't desirous of the bait, would you ever pursue it? Of course not.

Where do "desires" dwell? Inside of us. Our appetites, our emotions, our longings, our hungers.

You have just finished a big steak dinner with your favorite bowl of ice cream. You couldn't eat another bite. You then head out of the restaurant and a close friend approaches you as you are getting into your car and invites you over for a big barbeque at their home in 30 minutes. How much desire would surface under those circumstances? How much could your friend tempt you when your desires have already been satiated?

The word behind "desire" is *epithymia*, which is translated as "lust" 31 times and "desire" 3 times and simply means "a desire, craving, longing, mostly of evil desires."

It's important to recognize that temptations never seek to raise our desire for us to do good but only to do evil. You never are "tempted" to go and help a poor person, but you can be tempted to rob that person of whatever they have. God never limits our desires for good, nor does He make a "way out" of our desires to serve others. God intervenes only when a temptation seeks to lead us to sin.

This verse also reveals that these temptations specifically target our "own" desires and not anyone else's.

That's why two friends walking past the corner bar can be affected very differently. One person may not even notice the bar, while the other person who is a struggling alcoholic may immediately feel an overpowering desire to go in for a quick drink on the way home. Our desires are the root issue.

As John Owen once said, "There are many outward temptations that test men, exciting and stimulating them to do evil. But the root and spring of all these things lie in the heart. Temptations do not put anything into man that is not there already."

So, after being drawn away and having your desire piqued, what happens next?

Stage #3: Temptations increase their persuasive power by adding enticement.

"Each one is tempted when he is drawn away by his own desires *and enticed.*"

When we initially experience a desire for that which we have been drawn away to, often our desire is small and even minimal, just a slight pull. That's why the Bible adds the word "and." Temptations cannot succeed if the person only feels a small desire. Temptations need to raise that little desire into a compelling desire. Temptations build our desire with the third stage, by "enticing" us.

What is the purpose of enticement? To fan the flame of your desire so hot that it influences your thoughts and choices. As your desire grows stronger, you become less and less aware of anything else and become incredibly focused on the one thing you desire at that moment more than anything else.

But the truth is that only a few moments ago you weren't thinking about anything like that, were you?

The verb "entice" comes from *deleazo*, which means "to catch by a bait, to trick by alluring and enticements through deception." At this point, many of us fall prey to another major misconception because we think we are doing the enticing. But, once again, the verb "entice" is in the present *passive* form, which proves that you are receiving the action of another (temptation) and not actively doing the enticing. This fact is very important, as the temptation is the active worker in this biblical revelation; you are not.

So, guess what our experienced fisherman does? He knows that unless the fish's desire for that bait becomes stronger, the fish will probably never act and pursue it. The fly fisherman expertly hits that same exact spot in the river with the fly time after time—each time letting that fly sit on the water just a split second longer, increasing the likelihood that the fish will find the fly so desirous that he will break free from his inactivity and lunge for the bait.

Who is doing the act of enticing, the fish or the fisherman? The fisherman purposefully seeks to fan the desire of the fish over and over again. Never forget that you aren't fanning the flame of your desire—the temptation is! You may feel like you are growing your desire, but the passive participle proves that this is being done to you.

The fisherman seeks to trick the fish by deceiving them. The fisherman hid the hook very carefully inside the fly so that the fish would never think they are being pursued by their hidden killer.

Who would ever chase a dead piece of colorful string with a barbed hook hidden in it? Only a person who has been subtly deceived, convinced that this "fly" is not only real but that he must have it!

The temptation keeps the attention on how good that bait looks so the fish never has time to think about the potential dangers.

Enticing is cunning and artfully arouses hope of pleasure with no hint of any kind of danger.

Perhaps the clearest illustration of enticement in the Bible is found in Proverbs 7:

> There a woman met him,
> With the *attire of a harlot*, and a *crafty heart*.
> She was loud and rebellious,
> Her feet would not stay at home.
> At times she was outside, at times in the open
>   square,
> *Lurking* at every corner…
> With her *enticing* speech *she caused him to yield*,
> With her *flattering lips* she *seduced* him
>   (vv. 10-12, 21).

Temptations seduce us, just like the harlot. Temptations

dress up like an irresistible, juicy morsel for the fish. Temptations are crafty and lurk along our pathway. Temptations flatter. Temptations seduce. Temptations keep on enticing until they cause us to yield.

> We are no more responsible for the evil thoughts that pass through our minds than a scarecrow for the birds which fly over the seedplot he has to guard. The sole responsibility in each case is to prevent them from settling.
>
> **—JOHN C. COLLINS**

> You cannot keep birds from flying over your head but you can keep them from building a nest in your hair.
>
> **—MARTIN LUTHER**

The next time your desires are increasing, stop and realize: "The Harlot Temptation is seducing me! If I don't flee, I will likely yield and bite the hook!"

But is being drawn away a sin? No. Is desiring something that's clearly off-limits a sin? Never. Is strong desire for something off-limits a sin? Nope. Is the temptation successful yet? No, the fish is only feeling strong desire for the bait but hasn't decided to go for it.

Stage #4: Temptations continue enticing until your desire conceives a decision.

"Then, *when desire has conceived . . .*"

At this point, the analogy transitions from the stages of catching a fish in the first three stages to the four stages in a human life from conception to birth to maturity to death.

What is the major turning point in every one of your temptations? Your decision to sin.

After you have been drawn away, after your desires have been aroused, after your desires have been increased by various enticements, then the major turning point makes its appearance. You have no other option but to make a choice. When the enticement is at the highest peak, you are driven to make up your mind: Will you choose to sin or not to sin? Will you yield to your enemy or take "the way of escape"?

Your desires are emotions, aren't they? You "feel" desire; you don't "think" desire. As those desires escalate, as temptation fans the fire of your desire, your emotions rise up and seek to overthrow your mental decision-making faculties and your strength of will and spirit. Our emotions never decide anything; only our mind decides. But even if our mind decides something, our will must accept or approve that decision. Ultimately, the choice must be made by our will.

During this stage in our temptations, our mind struggles to find as many reasons to move forward as possible. These reasons are flawed, as they are only one-sided rationalizations. "Rational lies" are what we tell ourselves to justify our knowingly wrong intentions.

We avoid all thoughts of the painful and destructive results that will occur, and focus only on the pleasure and release we will experience. All these rise like a tsunami against the ultimate controller: our will. Our will can either accept or deny what our emotions and rationalizations are ganging up on us to convince us to act.

This internal struggle between our emotions, our thoughts, and our will may seem to go on for an eternity, but in most cases, the choice is made in only a few seconds, or a minute or two at most.

At that point of crisis, you must make a choice: to sin or not to sin. When you decide to allow your temptation to defeat you and you move forward and sin, then desire has finally been conceived in your life. As our amazing verses states, "Then, when desire has conceived." You are pregnant.

Temptations first get your attention (drawn away), then arouse your desire (emotions), then fan the fire of your desires to a higher level (enticement with rationalizations)— all for the ultimate purpose of overcoming your thoughts (mind) until you choose to sin (will).

If we return to our fisherman, when does the "conception" occur in the life of the fish? Keep in mind that, just like us, the fish were minding their own business until an outside influence, the fisherman (temptation), came along and followed some specific steps to catch the fish.

The moment of "conception" occurred the split second when one fish made the decision to swim for the fly floating on the water. Up until that moment of decision, the fish was safe and only considering his options. He ultimately decided that he wanted the fly more than anything else in his environment, so he prepared to act.

The enticement stage puts pressure on our decision-making thoughts until our emotional desires overcome our volition. The same Greek word translated as "conceived" in this verse is also used in Luke 1:24: "After this his wife Elizabeth became *pregnant* and for five months remained in seclusion" (NIV).

Did you recognize what caused the impregnation of decision? Not our enemy temptation. But as the verse clearly states, "When [our] desire has conceived." At this point, temptation must step aside as we are the only one who has the legal right to make the decision.

Our desire from the temptation overthrows our better judgment to do what is right, and we choose to sin. We cannot blame the temptation for this act, as the temptation only brought us to the critical point of choice. This can only be our choice, no one else's.

This fourth stage is the critical turning point for all seven stages in every one of our temptations. The first three stages all join forces to put as much emotional pressure as possible on the person to choose to sin, and the last three stages reveal the tragic results of that decision.

Stage #5: Temptations seek to push you to act on your decision and SIN.

"Then, when desire has conceived, *it gives birth to sin.*"

Stage five pictures the eventual result of our conception: We give birth to sin. When the verse states, "It gives birth to sin," we must understand the "it" to mean *our* desires, not the temptation's.

Temptations don't sin; we do.

The decision to sin in stage four nearly always gives birth to sin in stage five unless something quickly intervenes and stops it. The intention to sin isn't the same as the action of sinning. The decision to sin isn't sin yet.

It's critical to recognize that up to this point, *you haven't sinned*, but you are definitely heading in that direction with full intention.

As you will see in the final two stages, this verse builds on the analogy of human conception all the way through birth, maturity, and finally death.

But, like in all of life, a window of time exists between the moment of conception and the birth.

Sometimes the time between our decision and our sin is very short, while in other situations a more significant time period may exist.

For instance, let's say you are with your friends and everyone else is using heroin except you. Your friends all surround you, mocking and pushing you to join them. They promise a great high, and you are feeling alone and anything but high—so you make the decision that you are going to do it (conception). If the heroin is lying on the table, then the window between the decision and the birth of sin can be a few seconds.

But let's say that you are at a soccer match and those same friends circle you on the sidelines at halftime and push you to join them at the party afterward, and they want to know if you will join them when they take heroin.

If you agree at that time (conception), then you have the second half of the game, the drive over to the party, and right up until you pick up the heroin to reevaluate your earlier decision. You already know that your conscience and the Holy Spirit will strongly convict you to change your mind during the time between your decision to sin and your act of sin. The window of time between the decision and the act is when the Lord is bringing "the way of escape" right in front of you—all you need to do is not go with them after the game ends.

Until you take the heroin, you haven't sinned, and all of heaven deeply seeks your repentance. Repentance means that you change your mind before it is too late.

You have time to reconsider and abort your earlier decision. God desires this abortion. He wants you to change your mind before it gives birth to sin.

In this critical period, your emotions fight intensely with your will. Your feelings seek to overthrow your better judgment. All of us have experienced this struggle, haven't we? Sometimes we choose to abort, and other times we tragically choose to give birth and sin.

None of us look back to those times when we sinned with any degree of joy or happiness. Why? Because the consequences of our sin are always negative and destructive. But we also can look back at those times when we fought all the way to victory and feel relief and contentment, knowing God's pleasure at our victory.

Now you also know that God was directly involved with your struggle in four ways: First, God limited the power of your temptation. Second, God limited your temptation based upon your ability to fight it at the time. Third, God made the way of escape for you. And fourth, the Spirit of God strongly convicted you not to sin. Your inner conscience shouted at you, *Don't!*

If you decided to choose to sin and then sinned, then the verse describes you: "It gives birth to sin."

In the case of our fish, he has conceived and made the decision to eat the fly and waits with intense desire and built-up energy. The next time that fly hits the water, he springs into action and grabs the fly as he breaks out of the water. The crafty fisherman is beaming because he has successfully deceived the fish into biting a fake fly with a well-hidden hook. The hidden hook in the mouth of the fish is the birth of sin. He's hooked. He bit. He was fully deceived by his enemy. He lost.

The last two stages are the most serious and damaging to all of us. We are hooked, and if we don't get unhooked, our future can be very bleak.

Stage #6: Temptations accelerate in an area of repeated sin to form a sinful habit.

"Then, when desire has conceived, it gives birth to sin; and *sin, when it is full-grown*."

The fish now struggles because it has been caught—and swims wildly in the river as the fisherman reels in the line, embedding the hook more and more deeply into the fish's mouth. Over time, all the fish can think about is that hook and it desperately tries to get free, but the longer the hook remains in his mouth, the deeper it lodges and the weaker he becomes.

Sin is never satisfied, is it? The temptations have found a weakness, and they circle back on the person in the same area, time after time. Each time the person sins in that area, their resolve slowly weakens. If we have given into fits of anger time after time, our temper flares up quicker and quicker. At times we lose control and explode in anger. Rage begins to grow, taking more control of the person as we feed it by our choices. Verbal abuse and even physical abuse will likely follow in time. It will take less and less to set the person off into a total loss of control.

The term "full grown" is translated from the Greek word *apoteleo*, which means "to bring to an end, to accomplish, to grow until full grown." The word carries the idea of what happens when something is repeated over and over again until it is finished. This part of the verse alludes to the sad fact that if we continue in any given sin over and over, then that sin will grow stronger and stronger.

If the primary sin is greed and love of money, then the love of money grows until covetousness is all the person dreams of and works for. The insatiable quest for "more" becomes stronger and more addictive. Covetousness grows and puts pressure on the person to compromise in various areas of life as long as more wealth is gained. Relationships suffer as the addicted covetous person puts the pursuit of more money over all relationships. "White lies" eventually become the norm to keep the money rolling in. Sin is never satisfied with the same level of that sin for long, and it degenerates into deeper and damaging expressions. Sin grows until it becomes "full grown."

If the primary sin is pornography, then the person slowly over time gives in to those same temptations quicker and quicker. The former struggle, which was intense and perhaps extended, becomes shorter and shorter. The person becomes addicted in the full growth of sin and feels driven to find more opportunities and methods to watch pornography. They are not able to enjoy their spouse's sexuality nearly to the same degree as they were before they became addicted. Now all they desire is more graphic sexual pictures or YouTube videos for an ever-decreasing level of

THE TEMPTATION
KEEPS THE ATTENTION ON
**HOW GOOD THAT
BAIT LOOKS**
SO THE FISH NEVER HAS TIME
TO THINK ABOUT THE POTENTIAL
DANGERS.

satisfaction. The spiral down is tragic, and the person ultimately feels helpless to stop.

As you know, this period of becoming "full grown" is never quick but is extended. It takes time for the fish to tire in the fight until he can finally be simply pulled into shore without any more fight in him. No sin becomes "full grown" until we have chosen to sin over and over in the same area of our lives.

Finally, the final sad conclusion of this interaction of the pursuing temptation and the naïve fish occurs in stage #7.

Stage #7: Temptations dominate people by building a deadly lifestyle of bondage.

"Then, when desire has conceived, it gives birth to sin; and sin, when it is full-grown, *brings forth death*."

The fish struggles while hooked, but ultimately the fisherman pulls the exhausted and desperately weakened fish onto shore and his life is violently ended. Sin grows until death occurs.

How does this happen in a person's life? Sin grows in strength until that sin dominates that part of the person's life. After the domination, all temptation has to do is wiggle the specific bait for that sin in front of the person and the person will bite without even a struggle. That part of the person dies under the bondage of that sin.

The Bible reveals that on a human level, sin always seeks to dominate the person in that targeted area and then seeks to find other related areas to invade with new temptations.

The Bible repeatedly warns against falling under the bondage of sin. Look at Romans 6, which describes the "death" that occurs in all who would repeatedly give into the same temptation:

> Therefore do not let sin reign in your mortal body, that you should obey it in its lusts. *For sin shall not have dominion over you.* Do you not know that to whom you present yourselves slaves to obey, you are that one's slaves whom you obey, *whether of sin leading to death*, or of obedience leading to righteousness? For just as you presented your members as slaves of uncleanness, and of lawlessness leading to more lawlessness, so now present your members as slaves of righteousness for holiness (vv. 12, 14, 16, 19).

The further we moved down those predictable stages of every temptation, the more serious and troubling it became, didn't it? Who among us couldn't identify with our fish living through those universal seven stages of every temptation? Can you recall a time in the past or even the present when you were in bondage to a sin? How defeated and trapped you felt!

But, unlike that fish, which rarely escapes, the Bible has some magnificent good news for us. There's not only a way to spit out that hook and find freedom any time you choose, but even more wonderful, you can learn to discern when temptation's false bait first hits the water so you don't have to be fooled and deceived ever again.

Next we'll learn the final phase of our preparation for how to defeat your temptations time after time.

I've been so looking forward to writing the next chapter

that contains the Seven Tools to Defeat Your Temptations. Wait until you learn about the "Quick Spit" Solution, or the Bible Weaponized, or the Two-Minute Guarantee! If you are ready to enjoy much victory, just turn the page.

But always keep in mind: "No mousetrap ever holds free cheese!"

Watch and pray,

lest you enter into temptation.

The spirit indeed is willing,

but the flesh is weak.

MATTHEW 26:41

CHAPTER FOUR

The Seven Tools to Defeat Your Temptations

We've secretly invaded our universal enemy's territory with one goal in mind: to uncover the strategies that our enemy temptation uses on us so that we can defeat them. When you know exactly the steps your enemy will use before the attack comes, then you can much more easily defeat it. But just knowing what the enemy plans to do isn't the same as knowing how to use that information to defeat it.

The holy person is not one who cannot sin.
A holy person is one who will not sin.

—A.W. TOZER

Holiness is not freedom from temptation, but power to overcome temptations.

—G. CAMPBELL MORGAN

This chapter unveils a series of seven effective maneuvers you can take any time you are experiencing a temptation. Any one of them is effective all by itself, but if you use a couple of them at the same time, you will be much more likely to defeat your temptation quickly.

Never again will you wonder, *How did I give in to that temptation?* because you now know the exact process your temptation led you through, from one stage to the next. Therefore, never again lie to yourself about your temptations. Erase all these rational lies from your mind:

- It was just too strong; I couldn't help myself.

- I'm different; no one faces my massive temptations.

- It's in my family line—my "genes" made me do it!

- I've always done it—it's too late for me to stop now.

- The devil made me do it.

- I don't worry about temptations; I'm too strong. I have devotions every morning.

- It's not my fault; I was tempted beyond my ability.

- I prayed about the temptation but couldn't stop. God didn't answer my prayer!

- It's God's fault; He could have stopped the temptation from coming.

- Lay off—no one's perfect!

When temptations arise in your life in a new area of sin for you, you will likely go through the stages more slowly because you haven't lost to the temptations previously. But for sins you have committed numerous times, you will likely progress through those seven stages more quickly, sometimes seemingly instantly:

Temptation → Yes → Sin → Defeat

But perhaps for the first time in your life you have a very solid understanding of Temptation Territory. Now it's time to revisit what you learned in the previous three chapters with the goal of providing you with seven simple but powerful battle plans called "The Seven Tools to Defeat Your Temptations."

Temptation Tool #1: The Avoidance Technique

Temptation Tool #2: The Lookout Flare

Temptation Tool #3: The "Quick Spit" Solution

Temptation Tool #4: The Two-Minute Guarantee

Temptation Tool #5: The Weaponized Bible

Temptation Tool #6: The Pre-Commitment Declaration

Temptation Tool #7: The Call to the General

Three of these temptation tools are prayers to each member of the Trinity. The first is to the Father, the second is to the Holy Spirit, and the third is to Jesus Christ. Two tools utilize the Scriptures, and the other two focus on actions you can take yourself. The seven tools move from the easiest to the more challenging. These tools are not mere concepts but rather are power tools that anyone can use at any time and under any circumstance to gain victory over any temptation.

Tool #1: The Avoidance Technique

There's only one thing better than defeating a temptation: completely avoiding the temptation! This is the first of three tools that utilize your prayers. You have been instructed by Jesus to pray to God the Father so you can avoid a large number of temptations. To understand this prayer better, read what Jesus told His disciples to do in the Garden of Gethsemane the night He was betrayed:

> He came to the disciples and found them sleeping, and said to Peter, "What! Could you not watch with Me one hour? *Watch and pray, lest you enter into temptation.* The spirit indeed is willing, but the flesh is weak" (Matthew 26:40-41).

Jesus taught His best friends to "watch" and "pray" lest you "enter" into temptation. The disciples weren't experiencing any temptation at this point, but Jesus told them to pray so they wouldn't even "*enter* into temptation." Jesus told them to pray to avoid temptation! The disciples weren't asking Jesus to help them avoid temptations, but Jesus told them to pray to God the Father for this particular situation.

Jesus knew that although His disciples were willing, their

flesh was weak, making them extra vulnerable to fall under temptation. Did you catch the important connection?

Jesus told them to watch and pray so that they wouldn't fall into a temptation.

This secret is vastly underutilized by believers around the world because they don't recognize the power of their prayers in relationship to how many temptations they face. Could it be, my friend, that you have experienced far too many temptations simply because you haven't regularly asked God to keep you from them?

Not only did Jesus command His disciples to pray, but He also commanded them to "watch," and be on guard for the approach of any temptation. Jesus used the Greek verb *gregoreo*, which means "to be fully alert, to give strict attention, to be cautious, to be observant, and vigilant." The same word is used in 1 Peter 5:8: "Be sober, *be vigilant*; because your adversary the devil walks about like a roaring lion, seeking whom he may devour."

Both "watch" and "pray" are active imperative verbs, which means Jesus wasn't suggesting that they pay attention and pray in case they "enter into temptation," but rather He commanded them to watch and pray so that they wouldn't fall into temptations. Are you obeying Christ's command to pray lest you enter into temptations?

In the context of this verse, when Jesus commands us to "watch" and "pray," He is giving us the method to powerfully release God's help so we don't have to face temptations many times! Ask for God's help, especially when you are tired and weak, as the disciples were at that very moment. The more vulnerable you are at any given period in your life, the more likely temptations will come a knocking on your door.

Do you see what Jesus is revealing to His best friends? Up to that moment in the Garden, the disciples hadn't experienced any temptation, and Jesus didn't want them even to *enter* into any temptation. Why not? If there was no temptation, then no sin could occur! Remember, the Bible states you enter temptation only after you have been drawn away. The moment you are drawn away is the same moment you enter into temptation.

In case you are wondering if it is right to pray and ask God to keep you away from temptations, just consider this part of the Lord's Prayer in Matthew 6:13: "And *do not lead us into temptation, but deliver us from the evil one*: For Yours is the kingdom and the power and the glory forever. Amen." The same Greek word, *peirasmos*, translated as "temptation," is used by Jesus in the Garden of Gethsemane in Matthew 26 and also in the Lord's Prayer in Matthew 6.

When the disciples of Jesus asked Him to teach them to pray, of all the innumerable things He could have chosen to emphasize, He prioritized this one: "Do not lead us into temptation!"

Does God ever lead us into temptation? Absolutely. Why pray that God wouldn't lead us into temptation if He never did? And if your prayers to God to avoid temptation wouldn't work, then why did Jesus command His disciples to pray lest they enter into temptation?

You might need some additional proof as the concept is so far from our thinking. Look at this verse in Matthew 4:1: "Then Jesus was *led up by the Spirit into the wilderness to be tempted* by the devil." God the Spirit led Jesus into the wilderness purposefully to be tempted (see Mark 1:12: "The *Spirit drove Him* into the wilderness").

As you learned earlier, the Bible clearly states that God Himself tempts no one, but this passage proves at times God, for His own purposes, leads us into a season of temptation. How on earth can we bring these two clashing ideas into one unified understanding?

Unfortunately, we have strayed into some rather deep theological waters that would take far more development than this book permits, but perhaps a partial answer could assist you. The Greek noun for "temptation" in the Lord's Prayer is *peirasmos*, and the words "to be tempted" are from the verbal form of the same root word, *peirazo*.

As you previously learned, the same Greek word can have multiple meanings, depending on the context.

This one Greek verb *peirazo* also carries multiple meanings and can mean "*to tempt* to do evil" and also mean "*to test* to prove one's faith is strong and will successfully endure." (Note: If you reread James 1:1-15, you will find a very clear illustration of these two different usages [test or tempt] of the same word [*peirazo*] in the same paragraph.)

A temptation seeks an evil or sinful outcome, whereas a test seeks a positive outcome of greater strength.

God may lead us into a test, but His goal is always for our good, never for our failure, and certainly never for our sin. Instead, He tests us for many deep reasons, but each of them is rooted in His loyal love for us and His desire that we pass that test as a better, stronger, more committed follower of Christ.

The severest temptations that any of us face often occur during the last 25 percent of an extended, painful test. Our enemy is often directly involved in those times, seeking to push malicious temptations our way relentlessly, while our God is personally limiting those temptations based on our present weakened ability as well as always making the way of escape out of the temptation just for us. Both God and our enemy are highly motivated in the same situation, but for the exact opposite of results. God is using this test for our good, while our enemy is tempting us in our weakness to do evil.

In the Lord's Prayer in Matthew 6, Jesus was clear that He was talking about temptations, and not testings, as He finished the sentence about praying to God to "lead us not into temptation" with "but deliver us from evil" (v. 13 KJV). Jesus linked the prayer to not be led into temptation to evil, so that's why no Bible translates the Greek word *peirasmos* as "lead us not into testing" in the Lord's Prayer.

If you remember two of the many books I wrote, *The Prayer of Jabez* and *Beyond Jabez*, I commented quite a bit on the fourth prayer request of Jabez—"that You would keep me from evil" (1 Chronicles 4:10)—which is the identical idea as the Lord's Prayer.

The wise follower of Jesus realizes that God waits for your request to "lead me not into temptation" because that's very different from God's promise to limit your temptations when they come.

Isn't it so much better to have far fewer temptations than to fight so many of them? You have not because you ask not! So what's your action step? Start praying that God would keep temptations away from you!

Tool #2: The Lookout Flare

As you learned in the "Seven Stages of Every Temptation" chapter, every temptation transitions through the same seven unique stages from the beginning to the end:

1. To be *drawn away* from our current focus to the area of the temptation;

2. Arousing our inner *desire* for that sin;

3. Increasing our desire through various *enticements*;

4. The conception of the sin by our *decision* to sin;

5. The specific act of our *sin*;

6. The growth of that sin into a destructive *habit*;

7. The death of that part of our life that becomes a *slave* under the dominion of that sin.

The first three stages all build to the fourth all-important stage, your decision to give in to the temptation and commit the sin. The final three stages all increase the domination of that particular sin in your life.

Before explaining the Lookout Flare, I would like to encourage you for a moment. Whenever we think about our temptations and sins, it's never a very pleasant task. We must be on guard against feeling overwhelmed or discouraged in our fight against temptation and sin.

But none of us face temptations for 100 different sins, do we?! Absolutely not. Fifty different sins? No. Twenty-five? Highly unlikely. Read through the following list of 50 sins mentioned in the Bible for a moment and mentally check the sins you have been tempted to commit in the last year or so—but expect a big surprise!

Murder	Lying	Stealing	Adultery	Physical Abuse
Pornography	Drug addiction	Idolatry	Cheating on Taxes	Homosexuality
Swearing	Incest	Blaspheming	Gluttony	Witchcraft
Greed	Dishonoring Parents	Brawling	Cursing	Drunkenness
Unforgiveness	Covetousness	Bribery	Extortion	Slander
Envy	Lust	Jealousy	Astrology	Not Caring for Poor
Horoscope Reading	False Witness	Fornication	Denying Christ	Rebellious
Carrying a Grudge	Not loving spouse	Impudence	Kidnapping	False Teacher
Prejudice	Rape	Fits of Wrath	Rioting	Scoffer
Prostitution	Abuser of Self	Brawler	Hater of God	Occult & Sorcery

What did you discover about yourself? You may have been pleasantly surprised. Through testing this exercise with various audiences, the average person struggles with less than five types of temptations in any given year, many with three or less, and only a small proportion over ten.

You don't face temptations to sin in 50 different ways. Instead, your temptations probably focus on three to five sins that you have committed numerous times over an extended period of time. If you are strong in any given area, you will probably never face a temptation in that area.

When you overcome your temptations in any given area time after time, you will grow resolute and never even waver if you experience a temptation. For instance, when's the last time you were tempted to rape? Or bribe someone? Or practice witchcraft?

So, be encouraged! Your list of temptations isn't very long and can be overcome, one by one.

Remember Christ's command to the disciples to "watch!" lest they enter into temptation. You must be your own lookout, paying very close attention, especially in the first three stages of your temptation. Here's the powerful secret:

> *The earlier you discern you are under a "temptation attack," the easier it is to end it; the later you discern you are undergoing a temptation, the more difficult it is to end it.*

With that in mind, you can train yourself to pay closer attention to moments when you are distracted to another area of potential sin because you are being "drawn away" and the temptation is seeking to "overtake" you. What should you do when you discern that you are being drawn away to an area of weakness? Immediately send up a "flare" into your consciousness: *I'm under a temptation attack!*

Just realizing this is taking place and shocking yourself into awareness makes it very easy to immediately deny those thoughts and return to the matters at hand. You'll be amazed at how easy it is to defeat a temptation at this level.

But if your discernment missed that subtle distraction,

then you have already fallen into the arousal of your desire. Your desire is simply an emotion, an inner urge toward something God has clearly stated is off-limits for you. You can defeat the initial desire by instantly stating out loud, "No way! I found you out, temptation. I will not permit you to entice me one step further!" You must overcome your emotions at this moment or you know what's coming next: more wood on the fire of your desire through temptation's enticements.

As soon as you feel desire, pay attention, as your desire will likely increase with further enticements. Are you imagining? Are you wishing? Are you fantasizing? Are you remembering? As you practice paying attention, it won't take long for you to begin to discern quite easily that you have moved from "drawn away" and "desire" and are in the "enticing" stage. The sooner you can notice that, the easier it is to instantly stop your temptation dead in its tracks! Your action? Be on guard and send the Lookout Flare, "I'm under a temptation attack," and end it immediately.

But what should you do if you have fallen prey to being drawn away, your desire is aroused, and you are experiencing the rapid increase of your desire through various enticements? That's Tool #3, the "Quick Spit" Solution.

Tool #3: The "Quick Spit" Solution

I learned this secret while fishing with our son in a cold river in the mountains of Colorado. We hired a professional fishing guide one Saturday who brought his fly rods and handcrafted flies and drove us to the river he said was teeming with all kinds of trout.

David and I started fishing, and I set my fly right next to a little pool on the other side of the river—and all of a sudden the guide said, "You just missed one!" I was surprised and thought he was just joking with me, so I reeled in that fly and set it down a second time in the same place. "Yup," he said, "you missed another one!" David stopped fishing and started watching this little humorous escapade.

"I missed another one? What are you talking about— here, take my fishing pole and let me see you catch one of those fish I supposedly missed!"

Well, he took my fishing pole and expertly laid the fly right where I had been fishing and caught a fish! I couldn't believe it! By this time, David was sitting on the ground laughing uncontrollably as he watched his dad shake his head in unbelief.

Our guide smiled, handed me back the pole, and said, "You have to learn how to have a much lighter touch on the line—these fish have been caught dozens of times and thrown back into the river, as it's a 'catch and release river,' and they have learned not to bite the hook but just touch it with their mouth. If it's hard, they spit it out immediately."

He then smiled and promised we'd learn the required light touch by lunchtime. He was absolutely right. We did not catch any fish until after lunch, when we began to catch one after the other. You had to develop a very soft touch and discern that nearly instantaneous "nonbite" of the fish and catch them right in that instant!

The moment you recognize that you have started desiring something that is off-limits, practice the secret of the "Quick Spit" Solution and end the temptation instantly:

Immediately return to whatever you were thinking or doing before you were drawn away and consider laughing out loud! You foiled your temptation!

If you find out you are right at the edge of making the decision to sin, immediately recognize you have been tricked by your temptation! You've been fooled. Snookered. Deceived. A hook awaits you. You've bought the temptation's promise that only good things will result from your very bad decision!

Snap yourself out of temptation's clutches by stating the truth with internal fortitude: "This bait has a hook in it, and I'm not so stupid to think it doesn't! I choose to obey God!" If you are still weak, it means your desire has really been thoroughly enticed, so start listing all the reasons you can think of for not sinning and all the reasons why you will choose to obey. Remember, this struggle is nothing more than your desire fighting against your mind and will.

Choose to discipline your reckless desire quickly and forcefully.

If you decided to sin but haven't yet sinned, what should you do? Ask the Holy Spirit to powerfully convict you and arouse your conscience to come to your aid. The Spirit is always with you and will definitely come to your help. Remember, even though you decided to sin, you haven't yet! Calm yourself down, take a few deep breaths, and if you are still struggling, use the Two-Minute Guarantee, which is described next.

Tool #4: The Two-Minute Guarantee

Many years ago, when I was just beginning to understand these liberating truths about temptations, the Lord led me to a simple but powerful tool to help fight through my temptations. At that time in my life, I was leading a massive movement to the former Soviet Union with 87 Christian organizations and over 3,500 short-term and long-term missionaries. The stress, pressure, amount of work, spiritual opposition, cultural differences, and difficulties of operating across all ten time zones were depleting me to exhaustion. Temptations seemed to swirl around my life, and sometimes I felt weak and far too vulnerable.

Late one night while sitting in my favorite home office leather chair, I was complaining to God about the seemingly unfair competition between my enemy and my God. "How come," I argued with the Lord, "the enemy promises comfort if I give in to temptation and sin, but You don't seem to have any alternative to offer to help my distress?"

In one of those precious times when the Lord gives clear direction, He communicated that I was not using His solution for comfort. I struggled, reviewing everything I could think of, but I had no idea what God's solution was when I felt temptation. Then God communicated, "I gave you a person for the specific purpose of your comfort!" Like a bolt of lightning, I realized the answer had been right in front of me. Jesus specifically called the Holy Spirit the "Comforter" in John 14:26:

> *The Comforter, which is the Holy Spirit*, whom the Father will send in my name, He shall teach you all things, and bring all things to your remembrance, whatsoever I have said unto you (KJV).

The word "Comforter" comes from the Greek noun *parakletos*, which literally means "to be called to one's side

for the purpose of giving support and/or aid." In the widest
sense, *parakletos* signifies a "comforter," because the person
brought what we needed and we then enjoyed peace and
comfort. Whenever any of us receive whatever help or assistance we presently need, do we not feel comfort and relief?

The key to understanding this powerful secret is to recognize that "to be comforted" means that our emotions
become settled and peaceful. It doesn't necessarily mean that
the external problems have changed, but our emotional
reaction to those circumstances changed. We "feel" comfort;
we don't "think" comfort. Comfort isn't outside; it's within
us.

So I tried an experiment right on the spot. I put down
my Bible and simply prayed, "Holy Spirit, You were given
to me for comfort. I need comfort right now. Please comfort me!"

I don't know what I expected to happen so I just sat
there and waited. And then I became aware that I felt comforted. Really. At the same moment, all those irritating
temptations were nowhere to be found. As you'll see in a
moment, comfort doesn't leave any room for temptations!

What a magnificent revelation! God gave all of us a
priceless gift in the Comforter. Just like my wife can comfort me, so the Spirit of God who dwells within me can
grant me His gift of comfort. Simply because I asked for
His specific help.

Over the months that followed, whenever I felt discouragement, stress, or the presence of a temptation, I
immediately called for the Spirit's help. "Holy Spirit, You
were given to me for comfort. I need comfort right now.

Please comfort me!" Do you know what happened? Every single time, *without exception*, the Spirit comforted me and any lingering temptations quickly dissipated.

Then months later, I wondered how long it took for the Spirit to grant me comfort. So I took off my watch, prayed for comfort, and watched the second hand. Thirty-seven seconds and comfort arrived. I continued to test this time after time, and the Spirit gave me comfort between 30 seconds and always less than 2 minutes. Not once did I have to wait more than 2 minutes! Not the next hour, not later that day, not the next day—but less than 2 minutes.

What a wonderful gift! I then realized I only needed to hold on for less than 2 minutes and the comfort would flood my emotions and drive the temptations right out of my life. Who can't wait for 2 minutes?

I have shared this secret with thousands of people, and to this date many years later, everyone who has told me that they tried it agreed, "Comfort came in less than 2 minutes—and I didn't sin!"

You may be wondering how the gift of comfort relates to our temptations. As I taught on this subject, I began asking audiences how they felt right before they were tempted and sinned. In other words, what is the ground out of which most of our temptations grow?

I wrote on the flip chart their answers: "I felt discouraged, disappointed, lonely, not needed, a failure, physically exhausted, unhappy, hopeless, used, anxious, lost, or bored."

My next question was, "What did your temptation promise you if you would choose to sin?" The answers filled another flip chart page: "Relief, escape, release, rest, calm, pleasure, sleep, and I would forget all my troubles for a while and experience a little peace."

Those negative words describe how a person who is ripe for a temptation feels. Every single temptation offers something you desire at the time—and the most frequent desire is to escape the negative emotions and thoughts.

The lights went on in audiences all over because a major connection had been missing: the connection between negative feelings and the resulting surfacing of temptations. Our negative emotions of despair, discouragement, loneliness, failure, etc., are a massive void that temptations offer to soothe with a counterfeit answer: sin.

After numerous discussions with a large audience of businesspersons in Singapore, we all agreed that all those negative emotions could be best described by the "lack of comfort." That lack of comfort acts like a massive magnet or an empty void, pulling on anything that could promise a quick and satisfying amount of comfort, perhaps with some pleasure as the icing on the cake.

Every temptation, then, offers to give us comfort and supplies a quick release from all those negative feelings, even only for a short amount of time.

But when I asked the audience, "If you felt comfort and contentment instead of all those negative feelings, would you be internally driven to find comfort through a sin?" Everyone laughed because the answer was so obvious.

Did you make the connection? Comfort drives out the negative feelings that temptations must have to arouse your desire to sin.

You can use the Two-Minute Guarantee any time you

want. From lots of personal experience, I guarantee you nearly instant relief in less than 120 seconds. This secret won't solve the long-term underlying problem, but it will enable you to find comfort within seconds and therefore the inner push toward that comfort-promising sin will radically decrease and even end.

So why don't you use this tool? You won't be the first exception of it not working, my friend. The Holy Spirit is faithful and ever loyal to you. He is fully motivated to come to your aid when you are being tempted. When He gives you comfort, your heart is filled with joy and thankfulness because God the Spirit answered your prayer. And, unlike the enemy's temptations that always end in sin and bondage, the Spirit's comfort always brings joy and contentment.

But what can you do with those sins that are more deeply rooted in your life? How can you overcome those temptations that come with seemingly relentless pursuit? It's time to pull out a very big weapon!

Tool #5: The Weaponized Bible

The Bible reveals that there are at least four different sources of our temptations: our own flesh or old nature, the devil/Satan/demons, the world system, and other individuals or groups. It is beyond the scope of this book to discuss each of these sources, but each of these seven temptation tools work in spite of the source. The issue isn't where the temptation comes from but how to defeat that temptation.

We find another helpful tool to defeat our temptations in studying how Jesus defeated the powerful temptation from the "Master Tempter" himself, Satan. Jesus weaponized the Bible.

Look at how Jesus overcame Satan's onslaught: "And Jesus answered and said to him, 'Get behind Me, Satan! *For it is written*, "You shall worship the LORD your God, and Him only you shall serve"'…Now when the devil had ended every temptation, he departed from Him until an opportune time" (Luke 4:8,13).

Jesus defeated all three of Satan's deceitful, powerful temptations by quoting a specific scripture in direct opposition to the temptation. When each of the three temptations came at Him, Jesus repeatedly quoted the key passage in the Bible directly negating the temptation.

Each time He quoted the Bible, the temptation ended.

This strategy can be used any time you are tempted. But you must first identify the nature of each temptation and then state the verse either by memory or written on a card or paper you have with you to fight the temptation.

On a practical level, pick the area that you are facing temptations the most, and find one to three verses that state the biblical truth about that temptation, write them on a 3" x 5" card, carry them with you, and then when you are first sensing you are under a temptation attack, bring the card out and read it out loud if possible.

To strengthen the power of the verse, read it with your commitment to obey what the scripture states. Read it with your heart and energy behind it. Read it forcefully.

The Word of God is an extremely powerful offensive and defensive weapon! Stop leaving it on your shelf. Take it out of its scabbard and swing the truth and stab the lie right in the heart! Your temptation isn't your friend; it isn't neutral, and it is filled with a desire for your failure and destruction. Stop being a whimpering weakling. You are mighty in the Lord. Fight!

For instance, here are two illustrations of Bible verses that will defeat the temptations to worry or become angry or wrathful. For the temptation to be anxious or worry write these on a card and carry them around with you, reading them out loud if possible, the second you are tempted to start worrying:

> Be anxious for nothing, but in everything by prayer and supplication, with thanksgiving, let your requests be made known to God; and the peace of God, which surpasses all understanding, will guard your hearts and minds through Christ Jesus (Philippians 4:6-7).

> Finally, brethren, whatever things are true, whatever things are noble, whatever things are just, whatever things are pure, whatever things are lovely, whatever things are of good report, if there is any virtue and if there is anything praiseworthy—meditate on these things (Philippians 4:8).

(By the way, for more on this topic, see my book *Prayers for Freedom over Worry and Anxiety*.)

For the temptation to lose your temper or continue to be angry, here are some verses you could use:

> Make no friendship with an angry man,
> And with a furious man do not go (Proverbs 22:24).

Do not hasten in your spirit to be angry,
For anger rests in the bosom of fools (Ecclesiastes 7:9).

"Be angry, and do not sin": do not let the sun go
down on your wrath (Ephesians 4:26).

He who is slow to wrath has great understanding,
But he who is impulsive exalts folly (Proverbs 14:29).

A soft answer turns away wrath,
But a harsh word stirs up anger (Proverbs 15:1).

So then, my beloved brethren, let every man
be swift to hear, slow to speak, slow to wrath
(James 1:19).

Beloved, do not avenge yourselves, but rather give
place to wrath; for it is written, "Vengeance is Mine,
I will repay," says the Lord (Romans 12:19).

Now you yourselves are to put off all these: anger,
wrath, malice, blasphemy, filthy language out of
your mouth (Colossians 3:8).

You can use any Bible concordance and just look up the key word such as *worry*, *anxious*, *anger*, *wrath*, *adultery*, or *stealing*, and you'll find many verses to select and write on your cards. I have used this method numerous times over my life and found it very effective and ended the temptations in various areas, time after time. Just read the verses out loud right in the face of your temptations with your inner commitment, and they will flee.

There's the second half of this secret for those most difficult temptations that you have succumbed to far too many times in your life, the Pre-Commitment Declaration.

Tool #6: The Pre-Commitment Declaration

Sometimes the simplest answers to a problem can be the most effective. This temptation tool is a simple and quick solution that can be used any time during the seven stages of a temptation. This tool is very effective with your most difficult temptations.

This tool has two different parts: Part #1 is to write out in a couple of sentences stating your commitment not to sin the next time that specific temptation occurs; Part #2 is to read your commitment out loud the second you realize that you are experiencing that temptation.

Most people do not recognize the power of their pre-commitment. Undoubtedly, all of us have made promises to God after we have sinned and felt His conviction. But that commitment was made in a despairing moment and does not have the same power as a thought-through, written commitment.

The book of Daniel contains a number of illustrations of the power of the pre-commitment. For instance, when Daniel and his friends were tempted to break their obedience to the Bible, notice how quickly Daniel came back with a statement of their pre-commitment: "But Daniel *purposed in his heart that he would not defile himself* with the portion of the king's delicacies, nor with the wine which he drank; *therefore* he requested of the chief of the eunuchs that he might not defile himself" (Daniel 1:8).

This tool is to be used for an ongoing temptation in an area of your personal weakness or for areas in which you may feel you will face temptation in the near future. Find the verses in the Bible about your troubling sin as outlined in Temptation Tool #5, write them on your 3" x 5" card, and then write out your commitment on the back of the card.

The more you carry that card and read the verses and your own commitment not to sin in that area, the more power the truth will have over your struggles. Remember, the "truth shall set you free" is a universal truth, and the more you read and meditate on these scriptures and your statement of commitment on the back, the more your inner strength will grow.

Here's a sample to give you some ideas about an Anxiety Pre-Commitment:

> I recognize that my anxiety and worry is a sin. I confess I have sinned with anxiety and worry repeatedly in my life and commit, by the Lord's power, not to sin again with anxiety or worry. My anxiety is based on fear and God has not given me a "spirit of fear." I trust the Lord in this situation because His promise to me in Hebrews 13:5-6: "For He Himself has said, 'I will never leave you nor forsake you.' So we may boldly say: 'The LORD is my helper; I will not fear.'" I put my trust in the Lord and choose to thank Him for this test of my trust. I trust the Lord! I am fully committed not to sin with anxiety or worry. I choose not to sin with worry or anxiety!

And a sample of an Anger Pre-Commitment:

> I recognize that my extended anger and loss of self-control are both sins. I confess I have

sinned with my anger and lack of kindness and graciousness and am committed, by the Lord's power, not to sin again with anger, wrath, or losing my temper. I will not allow my anger to extend beyond one day. I put off my anger and my wrath right at this very moment. I affirm that a "soft answer turns away wrath" and that "a harsh word stirs up anger" (Proverbs 15:1). I choose to obey the Bible and will be "swift to hear, slow to speak, slow to wrath" (James 1:19). I commit to be kind to all under every circumstance! No person or situation "makes" me angry because I alone have chosen to respond selfishly in anger. I will no longer choose anger but wisdom and gentleness!

Read through the verses and your pre-commitment for whatever temptation may be hounding you, and I can promise that as you defeat them time after time, they will soon shrink back into the shadows. Over time your resolve will grow stronger so that you will eventually be free of those types of temptations.

Years ago, when I was struggling with one hounding temptation, I developed these two tools of Bible verses and my pre-commitment and began using my 3" x 5" card every time I felt my desire starting up to sin in that area (for me, it was anxiety and worry). I also put ten little boxes across the top of the pre-commitment side, and every time I used the card and defeated the temptation, I checked another box. Each time I read the verses and then with intensity read my pre-commitment, I found all my anxiety fled away. By the fourth time, I noticed that the temptations were quickly weakening (actually, they didn't weaken, but I became stronger in my commitment). I never got to check box #5. The temptations ended. Yes!

Never again think you cannot overcome your temptations! Each of these tools are powerful enough on their own to conquer any temptation you face. But just imagine using the Two-Minute Guarantee with the Weaponized Bible and the Pre-Commitment Declaration. Temptations won't have a chance.

But you still have one massive additional tool at your disposal. If you are a follower of Jesus Christ, your Savior and Lord, you can "Call the General."

Tool #7: The Call to the General

There's one Person who knows exactly how you feel when you are tempted, because He experienced the same temptations you have but successfully overcame them all. His name is Jesus Christ, and you know His temptations were far more powerful than any of ours because the great tempter himself, Satan, attacked Him with the most powerful temptations possible.

You have already learned the Temptation Tool #1 with God the Father in the Avoidance Technique and Tool #2 with God the Spirit in the Two-Minute Guarantee, and now it's time to learn Tool #7 with God the Son. Read carefully Hebrews 2:17-18 because Jesus wants to be invited to help when you are tempted:

> Therefore, in all things He had to be made like
> His brethren, that He might be a merciful and

> faithful High Priest in things pertaining to God, to make propitiation for the sins of the people. For in that He Himself has suffered, being tempted, *He is able to aid those who are tempted.*

Hebrews 2 states that because He was tempted like us, He is now a merciful and faithful High Priest for us. And, perhaps most important in this discussion, Jesus goes beyond just knowing of our temptations. The Bible says, "He is able to aid those who are tempted." If you ever wanted to talk to a person who knows where you've been regarding fighting temptations, then Jesus is your Person!

When the Bible states He is "able to aid" those who are tempted, what does this mean? The verb "is able" means to have all the power or authority to achieve the desired action. Because He is both our Mighty God and our merciful and faithful High Priest, Jesus has all power and authority available to Him, whether on earth or in heaven.

The verb "aid" is translated from the Greek word *boetheo*, which means "to run to give relief and comfort." *Boetheo* is a compound verb from *boe*, which means "a shout," and *theo*, which means "to run" for the purpose of assisting the person in need. The word captures the intensity of a "shout" with the intention "to run to aid" the person in need. When you call on Jesus, He shouts and comes directly to your aid.

Jesus leans forward in readiness to help you when you are suffering under temptations.

This passage also reveals what happens when we experience an extended period of temptation: "For in that He Himself *has suffered, being tempted,* He is able to aid those who are tempted." Jesus suffered while being tempted. In other words, the process of severe temptation can deeply affect the person in a strong, negative fashion.

Once again, the verb "being tempted" is passive, demonstrating that Jesus experienced the consequences of temptation to the point that He suffered. He felt deep pain during His intense struggle with His temptations.

Not only does the Bible teach that Jesus suffered great temptations and is able to help those who are going through their own temptations, but Hebrews 4:15-16 gives us an amazing promise we can claim time after time to ensure we come through our temptations victoriously:

> We do not have a High Priest *who cannot sympathize with our weaknesses, but was in all points tempted as we are*, yet without sin. Let us therefore *come boldly to the throne of grace, that we may obtain mercy and find grace to help in time of need.*

Not only does Jesus sympathize with our weaknesses and was tempted in all points yet without sin, but He wants to help us during our temptation so we won't choose to sin. Just think about that! The very Son of God stands ready and more than willing to help—but you must come to Him and ask for His help!

Did you pick up the common thread with all three tools related to God the Father (avoidance), God the Spirit (comfort), and God the Son (aid when tempted)? In all three cases, you must release God's involvement by praying for help.

Although God limits all your temptations and makes the way of escape without your prayers, if you don't ask God to help you to avoid temptations, to grant you the gift of comfort, and to come to your aid in a temptation, the God-head may not act in these additional ways.

Each one requires your dependence and humility in asking the Godhead for their help.

How should any of us feel if we come while we are tempted? The Bible, once again, shocks us with the instruction that during the very process of being tempted, we are to "come boldly" to the throne of grace!

This truth is one of the primary reasons why I wrote so extensively earlier that our temptations are never sins, just the doorway into sin:

> *Never allow any fragment of guilt or shame when you are tempted, or you will never be emotionally released to receive the benefits that these passages promise.*

Every member of the Trinity is directly involved in working for your victory over temptations—deeply desiring your victory, standing by waiting to be invited, and always ready to come to your aid.

These verses state that Jesus actively "sympathizes" with our weaknesses. He feels with you. He knows firsthand the suffering of extended temptations. What then are we to do about these matters? Because we haven't yet sinned and are weakening, Hebrews states, "Let us therefore come *boldly* to the throne of grace." Not with our heads down out of defeat but boldly and with great liberty, because we haven't sinned yet. The word "boldly" comes from the Greek noun *parresia*, which means "openly, courageously, confidently with all assurance, and without any reservation in our speech."

THE WORD OF GOD

IS AN EXTREMELY

POWERFUL OFFENSIVE AND

DEFENSIVE WEAPON!

STOP LEAVING IT ON YOUR SHELF.

TAKE IT OUT OF ITS SCABBARD

AND SWING THE TRUTH AND

STAB THE LIE RIGHT IN THE HEART!

When are we to come boldly into the presence of Jesus? These two verses are all focused on one specific situation in our life: when we are being tempted and need some supernatural assistance.

The logic is straightforward: Because Jesus was "tempted as we are, yet without sin" and because our High Priest "sympathizes with our weaknesses," therefore we have a highly understanding Person to ask for help.

The verse goes on to say that we should come to the throne of grace, that "we may obtain" something.

We are seeking to "obtain" something that we realize we cannot achieve without someone else's assistance. The word "obtain" means "to claim something for yourself, to take ahold of something that you can use." You are weak—you need inner strength and courage beyond your own resources. You need assistance from your powerful Savior.

The verse teaches we are to come to Jesus to "obtain" two different things that will help in our difficult temptations: mercy and grace. We need mercy to stop the temptation or at least weaken it further, and grace to bestow on us the added strength so we can finally overcome the temptation successfully.

As one who has asked for the mercy and grace from Jesus numerous times during painful testings and difficult temptations, I can promise you that this is one prayer Jesus loves to answer!

So what should you do the next time you are tempted to sin? Realize you haven't sinned yet and are completely innocent; therefore, come running to the throne of Christ and simply call out, "HELP!"

You don't need a long prayer—you just need to ask for one thing: HELP in the time of need! Ask and you shall receive!

Conclusion

We are now at the completion of the teaching portion of this book, and you are fully prepared to use the very helpful biblical passages and prayers for specific temptations that you face contained in the guided prayers portion. If you have read through these chapters with me, you know more about the truth of temptations and tools to defeat your temptations perhaps more than 95 percent of everyone you will meet. Because of this lack of awareness on how to overcome temptations, I chose to focus more in this particular book on the actual teaching. This is because I wanted to shape your mind-set on how you approach and view temptations. While prayer is a critical component to overcoming various temptations, so is the knowledge and understanding of what temptations are and how to approach them. It is my hope that this content will assist you as you go through the guided prayers but also equip you to pray your own prayers specifically related to whatever temptation you are facing.

After asking many people how much teaching they have received in their lifetime about the nature of temptations and how to defeat them, the average person quickly shakes their head and replies, "Well, I cannot remember ever hearing any sermon or small group on this topic."

But this book isn't produced for you just to know about temptations but to experience more and more victory over them. It is my heartfelt prayer that you will begin enjoying the freedom to walk in holiness in more and more parts of your life. Remember, however, from the first opening illustration of the pastor and young man that temptations will always be lurking around until you cross to the other side!

Until then, enjoy every single one of the temptation tools for your victory:

Temptation Tool #1:　The Avoidance Technique

Temptation Tool #2:　The Lookout Flare

Temptation Tool #3:　The "Quick Spit" Solution

Temptation Tool #4:　The Two-Minute Guarantee

Temptation Tool #5:　The Weaponized Bible

Temptation Tool #6:　The Pre-Commitment Declaration

Temptation Tool #7:　The Call to the General

Take the helmet of salvation,

and the sword of the Spirit,

which is the word of God;

praying always with all prayer

and supplication in the Spirit,

being watchful to this end

with all perseverance and supplication

for all the saints.

EPHESIANS 6:17-18

CHAPTER FIVE

Guided Prayers for Overcoming Temptation

Heather Hair

Now that you have a solid grasp on what the Bible teaches on the topic of temptation, the seven steps of every temptation, and the seven tools to defeat your temptations, it's time to focus our attention on prayers for defeating the key temptations that many of us face.

In the pages that follow, you will find considerable help and strength in using the guided prayers written by Heather Hair. You can either pray them in the order in which they appear, or you can select the specific prayers for the temptations you are currently facing.

The appendix, *Holiness Habits That Help Overcome Temptation*, presents practical steps to follow to strengthen your heart and mind so that you will gain additional inner strength to defeat your temptations time after time.

Achievement as an Idol

Dear Lord, You desire humility in my heart as I consider the things I have done in my life. This is because it is You who have moved mountains or opened doors, gifting me to live out achievements and dreams. Without You, I can do nothing on my own. This is why I pray against the desire of achievement rising so high in my heart that it becomes an idol in and of itself. While You have created me to accomplish great things according to the purpose placed within my soul by You, those things should never eclipse my right view of You as my Source of all things. Every good and perfect gift comes from above—from You, Lord. So help me pursue greatness in a spirit of humility and gratitude rather than from a heart of pride or need. My value and my worth are found in You, not in my accomplishments or in what others say about me. Keep this truth at the forefront of my mind as I walk in the expansion of Your favor and grace in my life.

In Christ's name, amen.

Entitlement

Gracious God, my heart betrays me at times as a spirit of entitlement creeps into my thoughts and emotions. This spirit prevents me from living in the somber gratitude that You desire me to have, knowing that it is Your goodness alone that supplies me with any good thing at all. God, You have blessed me with so much that I have never even thanked You for. Please bring to my mind all of the wonderful things You have provided so that I can thank You rather than become caught up in a spirit of entitlement. Teach me the virtue of surrender as I go about my days, and keep me from thoughts of expectation rooted in entitlement. I praise and honor Your name, Lord, knowing that it is Your kindness that supplies my every need and my wants.

In Christ's name, amen.

Lust

Heavenly Father, You have placed within me good desires for the wonderful things You have created for me to enjoy. But these desires can become corrupted when they morph into lust. Guard my heart from lust while maintaining my freedom to enjoy the pure and authentic desires You do allow. Please teach me how to enjoy all that You have freely given in such a way that allows me to feel satisfied and complete. In this way, my need to lust after that which I should not have or have not been given will diminish in the light of an awareness of all You have provided to me. Open my eyes to see all that You have supplied to me, and give me insight on how to pursue the attaining of that which You allow but that which I have not yet accessed or located, Lord. Remind me through Your Word about the dangers of lust giving birth to sin so that I will not sin before You.

In Christ's name, amen.

Pride

Lord God, Your Word is clear that pride is a terrible thing to hold in my heart and in my mind. It is the cause of the fall of Satan, and the cause of the fall of so many of us since him. Pride removes praise from our lips—praise that is rightfully Yours. Pride distorts worship and wonder. It removes gratitude and hinders love. Your Word states that authentic love never boasts. Lord, what can I truly boast about when You have supplied everything I need for everything I have done or have been? Pride is the greatest lie of humanity. Protect me from the temptation to sin in this way, but please do it gently, God. Guide me before the fall, for Scripture says that pride comes before the fall. Point my heart in the right direction without having to do so like a bridle in a horse's mouth. Open my mind and my spirit to discern Your leading so that I can turn from this temptation before it becomes a sin, which would carry the consequences of a heart lifted up against You.

In Christ's name, amen.

Willful Detachment from Loved Ones

Dear God, You have made it clear that there are two great commandments under which all other commandments rest. The first is to love You with all of my heart, soul, and mind. The second is to love others as myself. It is love that You have created me to live out with You and with others. But, God, as things have happened in my life that have wounded me, broken my trust in others, or disappointed me, I have found myself pulling back from this command to love freely and fully. Guard me from this temptation to cut off my heart from others. Guard me from a spirit that withholds love rather than gives it. Your Word says that when Sarah obeyed Abraham, she did so because of her fear of You. Help me to also love others because of my love for and trust in You. Let not any unwholesome words or thoughts about others lay claim to my life. Show me the rewards of loving well, giving me the courage to do so more and more each day as I put my trust and my hope in You.

In Christ's name, amen.

Love of Money

Heavenly Lord, surround me with Your protection as a bubble—a wall around me to guard my heart and my mind from the things that draw me into a love of money. Help me not to fall into the temptation of greed or materialism while simultaneously providing me with the freedom to enjoy all of the good things You have designed me to have. The love of money ought never to eclipse my love for You and for others. Give me insight into recognizing those times when it begins to battle for its position above either, and grant me the personal discipline and control to reign it in. I ask for reminders in Your Word as I read and spend time with You, meditating on Your Scripture to help reinforce the desire in me to keep money in its proper place in my life. Help me to be grateful for it, using it for Your glory and for others' good, and do not allow it to become an idol in my heart.

In Christ's name, amen.

Mismanagement of Money

Dear Lord God, the money You have provided to me has been given to me for a purpose. I am not unaware of the needs of those around me, including my loved ones, my church, and those around the world. While You own the cattle on a thousand hills and the earth is Your own, You have turned over the management of it to us—to me—as a steward. Guard me from frivolous spending. Keep my mind aware of those times when I am about to spend the money You have given to me on something that would be considered wasteful by You. Help me, rather, to use the money You have provided in a wise and effective manner. Thank You for all You have given to me. Show me the best way to use it. Keep me from the lust of the eyes and the pride of life that create in me a desire to buy more things that I may not even need, or to seek to impress people. Help me keep my eyes focused on You.

In Christ's name, amen.

Spiritual Apathy

Gracious Lord, there are so many things that compete for my attention. Some are entertaining. Others are simply distractions. Reveal to me the importance of spiritual awareness and attunement with You. Show me the power of abiding closely with You. Guard my mind from wandering when I spend time with You, Lord. I pray also that You will guard me from shutting off my heart from You as a result of pain, bitterness, or disappointment. Help me recognize that You have a plan and a purpose for the pain I've experienced in my life so that I don't run the risk of closing off my life from You to try and protect myself from future disappointment. Give me the spirit of wonder and amazement each and every day when it comes to You, God. And show me how best to have an ongoing relationship with You that brings me great joy and satisfaction.

In Christ's name, amen.

Selfishness

Heavenly Father, selfishness is at the root of all sins. It is when I cater to myself, my desires, and my interests first that I displace You from the throne of my heart. Sometimes living selfishly occurs so naturally that I may not even be aware that I'm doing it. Give me a heart like Yours toward my own selfishness. Break my heart, Lord, when it will enable me to become more pure in my devotion to You and to others. Burden me with Your view of sin so that I don't take it so lightly. I also pray that You will show me ways that I can serve You and others more continually in my choices and in my words. Make me an empowering force to those around me.

In Christ's name, amen.

Vanity

Jesus, You came as a humble servant on this earth. Scripture speaks of You as a man of no reputation. A man who would not be recognized by Your stature or by Your looks. And in this humility You gave Yourself to die for the sins of the world. You are the model of what it means to live without vanity. But Jesus, in today's culture, it is so easy to feel pressured to look a certain way, dress a certain way, or put on a certain look. In our social media craze we compare ourselves to others and focus more than we should on our looks and what we have. I pray that You will give me strength and personal discipline not to compare myself to other people. If need be, help me stay off of social media to the degree that it helps me to be content with who I am and how I look rather than allow it to drive me into a spirit of vanity. Let You be my model, Jesus, on what I should focus on in my heart and mind.

In Christ's name, amen.

Sexual Immorality

Dear God, thank You for the gift of sexuality. Thank You for the purpose of sexuality. Thank You for the desires and passions You have given to me. I ask that You will give me the grace to enjoy this gift of sexuality within the boundaries of morality as You've outlined in Your Word. Guard me from taking this gift outside of those boundaries in an effort to satisfy myself with things You have deemed to be harmful. Convict me, Holy Spirit, when I head down the path to sexual immorality—before my passions become so ignited that it is hard to pull back. Convict me early on, Lord, and set up guards around me to keep me from even heading that direction. I ask for Your greatest mercies in keeping me from the sin that is a sin against my own body, Lord. And I ask for Your greatest favor in discovering how fulfilling sexuality is within the boundaries You've prescribed.

In Christ's name, amen.

Worry and Anxiety

Dear Savior, I ask for Your intervention in my life when it comes to the temptation to worry or feel anxiety. God, I do want the strength to resist worry and anxiety, but I also know that You know I am but human, and when things cause me concern, that concern can quickly devolve into worry. That being so, Lord, will You please keep me from the things that cause me worry? Place Your angels of protection around me and my loved ones. Give me wisdom on what to put into my mind and what not to put into my mind, whether it's the news or movies or what I read. Help me think on whatever is pure, peaceable, and lovely. And station Your Spirit as my protection so much so that I am kept from much of what Satan would like to use to instigate worry in my heart. You are stronger than Satan and his schemes, Lord, and so in this area of worry I ask that Your strength will manifest itself in protection from this temptation.

In Christ's name, amen.

Habits of Procrastination

Dear Lord, You have created me on purpose and for a purpose, but that purpose will not carry itself out apart from my participation. You have never claimed that You will force me to live out Your will and destiny for my life. Procrastination is a tool of the enemy to keep me from doing the things I need to do in order to bring You glory and move forward in life. Procrastination is often rooted in laziness, so I ask that You will begin there by giving me wisdom on how to take care of the body You've given to me in such a way that I am living at my optimum level of energy each day. In this way, I won't be so prone to laziness and procrastination. Another reason why I procrastinate is having a lack of confidence in being able to complete the task at the highest level possible. Perfectionism is also a root of procrastination. Lord, help me be aware that it is truly Your grace that gives favor. Nothing I do is ever perfect. Rather, when I humbly offer my skills and gifts to You, You can build upon them to use them for Your perfect will. The results are ultimately in Your hands, God. Let this awareness of truth inspire me to start, and finish, all that I need to do.

In Christ's name, amen.

Overeating

Gracious Lord, You have given all good things for our enjoyment. This includes food. Food is not only needed by me for my nourishment and strength, but it is enjoyable and satisfying as well. However, moderation is a critical element in preventing me from eating too much and thus hurting my body as a result. I pray that You will teach me how to understand what my body needs and give me the wisdom to know what overeating can do to me so that I will understand why this temptation is so important to overcome. I also pray that You will give me joy in moderation. I don't need to limit my intake entirely or prevent myself from eating things I enjoy, but I do need to be sure that it doesn't turn into eating too much, which is the sin of gluttony. Forgive me for when I have binged on food or turned to food as a comfort rather than to You.

In Christ's name, amen.

Overspending

Dear Lord, make me aware of this temptation to over-spend before it becomes a problem or an issue. Bring this subject to my mind in ways that will disciple me into having Your mind-set on the matter. I thank You for the freedom to spend and enjoy that which You have given me. But help me be aware of the needs of others or the needs in Your kingdom that the finances You have given me could go to help. Also give me insight into the importance of saving for the future. Overspending creates a spirit of slavery to paying the bills or making more money. This is not the abundant life that Jesus Christ died to secure for me, so I reject the notion of overspending and ask for Your strength and power to maintain financial moderation in all that I do. Give me a quiet confidence in who I am and how You have accepted me—an understanding that my value is not dependent upon what I buy or do.

In Christ's name, amen.

Overuse of Social Media

Heavenly Father, You have created us for community. In fact, Your church is built on fellowship and communing with others. In many ways, social media allows me to stay connected to friends and family at a level that encourages community in so many ways. Yet as all good things usually do, it also carries with it a temptation to overuse it, waste time doing it, or allow it to disfigure my view of my identity in You. Knowing this is true, I'm asking You to help me keep social media in its proper place. Help me avoid the temptation to look to it on my phone before I roll out of bed, and even before I look to You or Your Word. Keep me from the reflex of turning to it in times of boredom. Rather, fill my heart and my mind with productive thoughts or simply a peaceful contemplation of my life in You. Make prayer as much a pull in my heart as is checking in on other people's statuses. Inspire within me a desire to check in with You over and above all else, Lord. Only then can I use this community tool in a healthy way that doesn't absorb both my thoughts and my time.

In Christ's name, amen.

Alcohol or Mood Stimulants

Holy God, I pray that You will break the bond alcohol or mood stimulants may hold on me. Tear down the chains that have led me to believe I am dependent upon them to get through difficult times. I pray for freedom from the pull to drink or the pull to pop a pill. Neither is necessary for me to live balanced, contented, and at peace. These stimulants are a roller coaster of ups and downs, creating an even greater dependency in that cycle itself. Please, Lord, break me free from this. I am a blood-bought child of the King, and I have been set free from the ties that bind me to alcohol or mood stimulants of any form. I can do all things through Jesus Christ who gives me His strength. He is my healer, and by His stripes I too am healed. I am trusting You, Lord, in these truths each and every moment of my days and nights, knowing that it is in Your truth that I am set free.

In Christ's name, amen.

Emotional Affair

Dear Lord God, guard me from the temptation to have my emotional needs met by someone who, from Your perspective, shouldn't meet them. Guard me from looking to someone whom I shouldn't in ways that stretch outside the emotional intimacy prescribed in marriage for a couple. Whether the other person is married or I am married, or both, open my eyes to recognize the dangers of allowing and nurturing an emotional attachment to another person in a way that violates the bonds of a covenantal love that has already been established. Even more so, help me not be a temptation to someone else. Help me encourage others, yes, but not in such a way that lures them into desiring more from me emotionally than would bring You glory and would honor the covenantal bonds already existing. Show me the dangers of these types of emotional affairs before I am in too deep so that my eyes can be opened and my feet can run free before any damage is done to loved ones, or to each other.

In Christ's name, amen.

Pornography

Heavenly Father, set me free from the illicit pull of sexually gratifying myself through watching others engage in sexual activities in pornography. Let those moments when I give in to the temptation bring a deep emptiness to me that awakens me to the damage I am not only causing myself but my loved ones. Educate my mind as to how dangerous pornography is to my real-life relationships. Break the yoke that binds me to this perversion and do it immediately. I trust that Your strength will be enough for me to be set free. And show me in the ways that only You can how You do provide sexual satisfaction through marriage and the moral boundaries You've outlined in Your Word. Help me discover these pleasures at a greater level than I ever have before and to take delight in them.

In Christ's name, amen.

Personal Blame and Shame

Heavenly Father, lead me away from feelings of personal blame and shame and into the truth that there is now no condemnation for those who are in Christ Jesus. Help me not to look at my own unrighteousness and sins I have committed but rather to trust in the complete and perfect righteousness of my Savior, Jesus Christ. Cover my emotions with His blood as You have covered my sins so that my emotions align with Your truth in every way. When thoughts of personal shame or blame present themselves in my mind, enable me to recognize them for what they are—a tool by the enemy to draw me into this temptation. Enable me to cast them down immediately before they have an opportunity to take root and flourish into thoughts of my own. Make me mindful of Your grace and mercy so that I may go boldly to Your throne in prayer during times of need. Rather than seeking to cope with personal blame or shame by adding more shame through actions that displease and dishonor You, give me the ability and wherewithal to praise You in those times. Help me flip this temptation into a victory each and every time Satan brings it my way.

In Christ's name, amen.

Self-Pity

Gracious God, You know the things that have happened to me. You know the pains I've had to bear—the difficulties I've had to overcome. But just as You were with Joseph in the pit and later in the prison, I'm asking You to be with me in my darkest times so that I don't fall into a spirit of self-pity. I'm asking that You will give me the wisdom to view the challenges I've faced and trials I've overcome with an eternal mind-set. Help me not to fight against the development You have sought in my own spiritual life through these valleys, but rather to participate in and embrace it. Let Jesus be my guide, as He did not fall into self-pity when the sins of the entire world were upon Him, mine included. And rather than call ten thousand angels to set Him free, He surrendered His will to the higher purpose You had in store. Let me overcome this temptation in like manner, bringing good to others and glory to You through what You are accomplishing both in and through my life.

In Christ's name, amen.

Unforgiveness

Dear Lord, I come to You with a heavy heart, burdened by the weight of unwanted bitterness. I do not wish to carry around and harbor hurt emotions. I want to be free from the things in my past that have wounded me. Transform my mind to see these things through Your eyes. Help me recognize their purpose. Help me, like Job, discover a heart of compassion and awe for You to such a degree that bitterness and unforgiveness toward those who have mistreated me cannot even begin to take hold of me. Release me from the temptation to remain angry and withhold forgiveness to others. And surround me with blessings of peace that reach beyond my own personal understanding of how I could be feeling it. Let me marvel at Your care to such a degree that the temptation to hold on to unforgiveness becomes entirely distasteful to me.

In Christ's name, amen.

Lying

Gracious God, in You is truth. Your Word is truth. You are the Author of truth. In You is found no deceit. You have called me to be holy as You are holy. When I lie, I am serving the father of lies—Satan—and not serving You, my Savior. Give me a quiet confidence in the truth of my life—the truth surrounding my achievements, my actions, and my outlook. Help me not to be drawn to manipulating circumstances and people through untruth. I desire to be free from the power of deception both done to me and through me, and thus I ask for Your strong and mighty hand to deliver me fully. Show me the beauty of truth and grant me favorable responses from those around me in order to reinforce my longing to speak truth and be comfortable with speaking truth. I praise You and thank You for abiding deep in my spirit with Your Holy Spirit, convicting me when I am telling lies or about to do so.

In Christ's name, amen.

Laziness

Heavenly Lord, You have called us to come to You for times of rest. Jesus spoke that those who are weary and heavy-laden can find rest in You. Jesus Himself frequently went away for times of rest and reflection. Yet laziness is taking a good thing—rest—and indulging in it beyond what is considered rest and needed for restoration. It involves morphing it into a state of sluggishness and unproductivity. Because even in Jesus's rest, He abided with You as we are called to abide in Him. Give me wisdom to discern between rest and laziness. Give me self-control not to allow myself to give in to feelings of laziness. Surround me with role models who know how to use their energy in a healthy way but who also know how to rest well so that I can see what true balance looks like. And keep me from the temptation of overworking myself so much that I then plunge into laziness as a way of escape. Thank You for the energy supplied to me through Your Son.

In Christ's name, amen.

Judging

Dear God, an awareness of my own personal sin is the first antidote toward the temptation to judge others. An awareness of all that You have forgiven me of and withheld judgment from me is the first level of protection against the temptation to judge others. I pray that You will keep me aware of the depth of Your great grace and mercy toward me, and Your compassion—not so that I feel shame about it—but so that I can and will extend that same grace, mercy, and compassion to others. While their sin may be in a different category than mine, all sin is equally detestable to You. Keep me in a spirit of humility, Lord, so that haughtiness doesn't draw me into judgment. After all that Jesus did to save me from my own sins, let me not belittle that sacrifice by saying it doesn't apply to all others. Keep me from the temptation to judge, Lord, so that I do not sin against You.

In Christ's name, amen.

Holiness Habits That Help Overcome Temptation

The serene, silent beauty of a holy life
is the most powerful influence in the world,
next to the might of the Spirit of God.

—BLAISE PASCAL

Back at the turn of the century, Samuel Smiles expressed the theme of this chapter:

> Sow a thought and you reap an act; Sow an act and you reap a habit;

> Sow a habit and you reap a character; Sow a character and you reap a destiny.

This life-linkage is unmistakable and unbreakable. We move from thought to act to habit, and those habits create our character. Never in your life are these steps out of order; never are they skipped. Ultimately, your destiny is controlled by the habits of your life and thoughts. Right smack in the middle of that five-link chain (thought to act to habit to character to destiny) is the concept of "habit." A habit of life is a settled tendency or usual manner of behavior that has been acquired by frequent repetition over time so that it has become nearly or completely involuntary.

"When a habit is built, a character is formed." When you think about it, character is the sum total of a person's habitual traits and qualities. When a major habit changes, that part of the person's character changes. For instance, if a person habitually lies, his character becomes untrustworthy. If he learns to habitually tell the truth, his character becomes fully trustworthy.

Let's say you are at a company party and one of your coworkers is behaving totally out of the norm. In describing her behavior to her perplexed boss, you say she was acting "out of character," which means she was not acting the way she habitually acts.

> *Change your habits and in time, you will change your character. Therefore, to enjoy a life of holiness, change your habits into habits of holiness.*

If you want to become a person whose character is holy, then you will have to identify and establish personal habits of holiness. The longer and deeper those habits are practiced, the more they will become a part of you—until finally they become the "whole" of you! Habits which become involuntary are called "character qualities."

When people seek to change their character, they must change their habits. To move from unholiness to holiness means, at least in one sense, habits of life have changed from negative habits of unholiness to positive habits of holiness. When they seriously pursue holiness, the reality of what becoming holy means must move beyond the generalities into specifics. Holiness isn't some vague dreamlike existence painted with a soft, glowing aura of heavenly clouds. Holiness is specific and objective and is to be fully mastered by all who name the name of the Lord Jesus. The Lord calls us to be holy in all our conduct (1 Peter 1:15), and He has provided everything we need for righteousness and godliness.

Because the Bible teaches that holiness is both a *position* as well as a *progression*, we must continue to think clearly of how holiness really works. Holiness begins the moment we accept Jesus Christ as our personal Savior. At that time, the Lord separates us unto Himself as His child and a member of His family. From that point forward, the Lord calls all of us to be transformed from glory to glory into the exact image of Jesus Christ (2 Corinthians 3:18). As time goes on, all of us should be exemplifying the traits of Christ's character—love, joy, peace, longsuffering, kindness, goodness, faithfulness, gentleness, and self-control.

> "Holiness does not consist in mystic speculations, enthusiastic fervors, or uncommanded austerities, it consists in thinking as God thinks and willing as God wills."
> **—CHUCK COLSON**

Although our lives may demonstrate seasons of holiness acceleration for most of our lives, growth will be gradual and steady. Just as none of us can actually see the growth of a nearby plant or flower as it occurs, yet if we leave for the day and come back in the evening a bud may have opened into a beautiful rose, so is our growth in holiness small but significant. Leave time for its natural growth, and you'll see a noticeable difference. In 2 Corinthians 7:1, Paul reminds us that we are to "cleanse ourselves from all filthiness...*perfecting holiness* in the fear of God." "Perfecting holiness" reflects the lifelong process of conforming ourselves into the image of Christ.

Remember, habits determine character. Character is not transformed unless habits of thought, belief, and behavior are changed. As you change your habits, your character will also change. You won't have to "hope" that somehow, in some way, your character will change, because you know it will change. Not instantly, but certainly. As you can't see that rose open its petals, so you won't be able to see your character blossom into Christ. But, circle back on your life in a few months, and you may not recognize yourself!

How is it possible that holiness will result from these habits? Because the Bible repeatedly exhorts us to practice them—often with specific promises and benefits tied to them. Throughout the history of the church, Christians just like you and me have practiced these habits and have always enjoyed the same beneficial results. You don't have to hunt around for some magic words or secret initiation rite—these habits are obvious and equally within reach of all of us.

Try this experiment: Think of the most godly person you have ever met. Call him up and tell him you are reading this book and that I encouraged you to call and ask one question: "What have been the three secrets of your walk with God and godly lifestyle?" If my experience reflects the norm, you'll find they are the same main spiritual disciplines outlined in Scripture. Don't expect something new or exotic. Most importantly, you can only expect things to make a dramatic difference if you practice them regularly over a long period of time.

Holiness Habit #1: Establish Your Devotional Habit

What is currently the center of your life? Your work? Your marriage? Your family? Your church? Your leisure? Your money? Your business? Whatever is at the center of your life, you must move it into second position so the Lord and your time with Him reigns as the central focus of all that you do. The single most strategic change you can do to sow seeds of holiness and later reap holiness is to put your daily devotional habit first on your priority list at this very moment.

Half of the devotional habit is the word *devote*, which means "to set apart for a special and often higher end." The focus of daily devotions isn't the specific procedures one follows, but one's intimate relationship to the Lord. Because you are devoted to the Lord, you choose to dedicate priority time each day to Him and Him alone. And because He is the most important person in the world to you, you do not allow anyone or anything to take precedence before Him.

Here are a few tips to maximize your devotional habit.

Select Your Devotional Habit Place

The first key to successful devotions is to identify your favorite location in the house for your devotions. It should be comfortable, absolutely quiet, and as private as possible.

In the Wilkinson home, "Darlene's Place" is in the front room in her green rocker, "Jessica's Place" is in her bedroom, and "Bruce's Place" is in the basement, in the back corner overlooking the backyard.

In that corner sits my favorite blue chair a good friend from Colorado gave to me unexpectedly one afternoon. Just in front of it along the wall is a bookcase filled with my "spiritual life" books, more recent journals, and my prayer journal. To the left is a lamp with a small table and at my right a large globe for praying for the world. For me, it's perfect.

As time passes, I have set apart this space to the Lord and dedicated it as the place where I rise to meet Him in the early morning. This place has become filled with praise, worship, meditation, and intimate friendship.

Schedule Your Normal Devotional Habit Time

I grew up as a staunch evening person. I was sure it made no difference to the Lord what time I decided to have my devotions, and I can remember defending my position rather vigorously in my early Bible college days. One day many years ago, an older mentor and I were bantering this question around and he asked me if the spiritual giants of history had their primary devotions in the morning or evening. I had to admit that every one of them I was familiar with had them in the morning, but I was quick to point out that didn't prove anything.

When I said that, he folded his arms, smiled, and just sat there—not saying a word. Finally, when I had nothing else to say, he warmly but soberly said, "Bruce, until you stop defending your laziness and rise with the sun, you'll never meet Christ as you are seeking Him." With that, he rose and left.

> "The greatest miracle that God can do today is to take an unholy man out of an unholy world, and make that man holy and put him back into that unholy world and keep him holy in it."
> **—LEONARD RAVENHILL**

That friend proved absolutely correct. The early morning hours are the *holiness hours*. Over time, things changed and I have become a committed morning person. The Lord and I like to meet while the sun is yet rising to join us.

This may mean you will have to alter your routine, get to bed earlier, or at times live with less sleep. In most people's busy lives today, when priorities change such as this, sleep suffers until you learn to discipline yourself a bit more closely. Whatever you eventually decide, *meet the Lord at the same time each day throughout the week*. As far as Saturday and Sunday are concerned, you should set realistic times on these two weekend days. Personally, I don't get up early on Saturday, but do most Sundays. Saturday frequently permits a more casual approach, and I'm not unsure that the Lord doesn't enjoy this leisurely approach as well.

Remember not to fall prey to the temptation to become legalistic in your walk with the Lord. Your devotions should flex with the ebb and flow of your life, including emergencies, exhaustion, and unexpected situations. One weekend while ministering at the Billy Graham Cove in Asheville, North Carolina, I found myself counseling all day and very late into the evenings. On the last morning I was so emotionally and physically exhausted that I rose early Sunday morning, pulled a large stuffed chair up to the fireplace, and enjoyed the presence of the Lord in quietness. I didn't follow my normal schedule, didn't pray through my prayer list, didn't write in my journal, and didn't even read my Bible. What did I do? I just sat in the presence of the Lord for an hour—worshipping and enjoying Him. Remember, devotions are for man, not man for devotions.

Structure Your Normal Devotional Habit Agenda for Each Day and Year

Nothing seems to ruin good intentions faster than not knowing what to do when you semi-stagger in the early morning hours to your devotional place—and then spend those precious moments in frustration trying to figure out what to do.

Take the complexity out of life! Build a routine that you follow each morning. I have discovered that the best way is to construct a new routine for each year from what I discovered during the previous year. Then, when I finally sit in my big blue chair with my orange juice and coffee, I don't waste a second. It's wonderful, but unfortunately, I have to admit that it took me years just to figure that out. I can still remember the frustration of searching through the Bible trying to figure out what to read, or what to pray, or just to get started. Now that never happens. As I said, it's wonderful!

> "The chains of habit are too weak to be felt until they are too strong to be broken."
> —SAMUEL JOHNSON

What's the secret? Just figure out what seems to work for you right now—write it down on a card or sheet of paper, try it the next day, and revise it. The first time it may take a couple of weeks to really zero in, but relax and don't try to figure it all out the first time. Get started and then revise your list of steps until you are comfortable; then use them for the rest of the year. The point isn't how many things you do, but that whatever you do works for you.

Tips for Success

The first thing you should do is the easiest, most motivating, and the thing that starts your engine best. Never tackle the hard things first, but prepare yourself. For instance, one of my wife's friends starts her morning by turning on a praise tape, closing her eyes, and worshipping the Lord for as long as she desires. For me, I read a spiritual biography or spiritual life book for a while—it gets my battery charged. Remember, the key is to start with whatever you find is the easiest, most enjoyable and immediately encouraging. There's nothing more spiritual than to immediately start praying first. If I started with prayer, I'm afraid I might fall back to sleep! Darlene, however, starts her morning with prayer and praise, then reading her Bible, then her journal, and ends with additional prayer. The order isn't important to anyone but you.

Second, when you are ready to turn your heart toward the Lord, stop yourself, and prepare yourself for Him. Close your eyes and quiet your heart. Bring all your thoughts into sharp focus upon the throne room in the heavenlies. Bring every thought captive and do not permit interfering or distracting thoughts to conquer your intention. If this is new to you, you will become more than a little frustrated as your mind seems to be like our new, untrained little puppy, yipping and running in every direction at once. For the first few months, this may take more than a few moments, but don't become frustrated. Eventually, bringing your heart into focus will only take a few seconds.

Third, follow your schedule point by point in the same order every day. Don't skip a step, no matter how much you're tempted to do so. Discipline yourself and do not permit the "avoidance temptation" to conquer your resolve. This avoidance emotion can be quite strong, but must be conquered. Put your finger on the step you're working through in your devotions and don't move onto the next step until you have finished that step. When this happens to me, I take careful note of it and mark a little star in the margin to alert me to the spiritual opposition.

Whatever you do, don't permit your focus to leave the Lord and what you are committed to doing in this devotional step. As you remain focused on Jesus Christ, the opposition will always dissolve shortly right in front of your eyes. Don't doubt this principle. Just this morning on number 16 of my prayer list, I unexpectedly experienced this very thing and remembered that such opposition had occurred yesterday and the day before that. Why? I don't know, and don't necessarily need to know—so I upgraded my fervency and broke through. Tomorrow I'm going to come to this step with commitment and dependence upon the Lord that the opposition will flee into the darkness.

Fourth, don't ever allow anything to take the place of the

two absolutes: prayer and the Word of God. Never allow any book, no matter how good, to take the place of reading His Word. Never allow yourself to skip or shorten the amount of time you pray before the Lord. Regardless of what you do in your devotional schedule, at least 50 percent of your total time should be focused on the "Big Two"— prayer and the Word.

Why not spend a moment, take a piece of paper, and develop your first devotional schedule right now? Start revising it after you try it tomorrow morning. If it's your first year, don't try more than three or four or you'll be exercising with weights that are too heavy for you. Value the habit more than the difficulty or depth at this point! Take these basics and put them in the order you think you would enjoy them best:

Bible reading

Prayer

Praise and worship

Journaling

Reading a Christian book

What happens if you miss a day? Or a week? Or even a month? Prepare yourself to restart this holiness habit and pick up exactly where you left off. Don't try to catch up— just skip what you missed. Never permit yourself to construct a mountain you must conquer to make yourself "pay" for neglecting the Lord. Christ paid for all your sins and all of mine. His payment was sufficient for the Father, so it also must be for you. Just apologize to the Lord as you would to another friend for avoiding their company and receive His forgiveness and warm embrace. He's missed your fellowship more than you missed His. Remember, no relationship flourishes long term if it is based merely upon guilt and responsibility.

Holiness Habit #2: Meditate on Scripture

Of all the specific holiness habits which build holiness and directly control your transformation into a person of holiness, reading the Word of God is the absolute highest priority. Although you may think that prayer is the secret to transformation, I do not believe the Bible teaches that. Rather, the Bible is the *primary transforming agent*. Obviously, the Holy Spirit is the ultimate transformer, but He uses the Word of God as His primary tool of transformation. Notice how the apostle Paul describes this transformation in Romans 12:2: "…be transformed by the renewing of your mind." Transformation begins with the believer's mind, not his behavior. All of us behave exactly in accordance with what we believe. Although we may think our behavior doesn't reflect what we deeply believe, the Bible reveals it does. In fact, there is never an exception.

If I sin, then at the time I sinned, I thought that, considering all the options, sinning would be in the best interest for me, or I wouldn't have sinned. When I truly believe that the best option for me is obedience, then I will choose obedience.

What I think determines what I do. What I believe determines how I behave. Since that is true, the critical issue is for my mind to be changed to think exactly what the Bible teaches. Usually, our minds are not changed instantly nor in a sudden flash, but little by little as we understand and believe more and more of the truth.

Paul revealed that transformation is a process by his choice of the word "renewing" (Romans 12:2), which literally means "to make new again" and again and again. The believer must make his mind new over and over again until every thought from the old ways of thinking have been rooted out and everything from the new (biblical) way of thinking has been firmly planted and rooted.

Transformation occurs by *renewing our mind* by the Bible and not merely by reading our Bible. Although reading the Bible certainly influences our life in many wonderful ways, our transformation only occurs as our mind is changed from believing a lie to believing the truth. If reading the Bible doesn't adjust the way we think, then the Bible won't magically transform our behavior. Never forget those famous words of D.L. Moody, "The Bible wasn't given for our information, but our transformation." Don't read the Bible only for information; read for transformation through the renewing of your mind.

Renew Your Mind by Reading the Whole Bible or New Testament Each Year

The habit of reading through the Bible or New Testament every year is a wonderful practice that hundreds of thousands of committed believers practice. There's nothing better for general spiritual vitality than reading through large passages from the Bible day after day.

Renew Your Mind by Meditating on Carefully Selected Verses

Unlike reading through large sections of the Bible, this habit carefully selects small passages which focus on those areas of your life that you know need to be transformed in order to fully please the Lord.

How do you know which verses to meditate upon? Watch your behavior and monitor your attitudes, and whenever you find anything that isn't duplicating Jesus, that's your meditation agenda. Take that area of your life and find three to five different verses or sections in the Bible that deal directly with your problem area.

Type or write out these verses on some 3" x 5" cards and start reading them out loud day after day. Dedicate at least one month to each area, as you'll not be able to renew your mind fully within only a few days. Slowly meditate on these verses while asking the Lord to show you where you believe the lie that must be discarded and the truth that must take its place.

Each time you read these verses, put a mark on the bottom of the card and stay on target until one of two things has happened in your life. If you uncover the lie you believed was the power behind your sin, carefully and actively renew your mind in that area until you know your mind has changed and you see reality differently.

If your cluster of sins surrounding that particular lie is no longer a part of your life, you can stop meditating, as you know your transformation worked! The point of scriptural meditation isn't that you meditate, but that you are completely transformed in that particular area. The process is only valuable to you, therefore, to the degree which it brings transformation to you!

So many well-meaning believers memorize Scripture without any transformation, thinking that somehow if they can just remember the verses, the transformation will automatically and supernaturally take place. Some of the most carnal Christians I know can quote the most scriptures by memory! Memorizing scriptures only puts them in your memory bank so you can meditate upon them with the goal of being transformed by them. If memorization is viewed as the desired target, then memorization becomes an end in itself rather than the means to the biblical end of transformation.

If you truly want scripture memorization to transform your life, select an area of your life which you know needs transformation. Name that area needing transformation with a biblical word, such as anger or stealing or lust or gossip. Then find the best three to five passages in the Bible about that area which give clear statements of truth and directives for life, and write them down on a 3" x 5" card. Carry these cards with you everywhere and read them out loud over and over again. Think through every single word and seek the wisdom that lies within those verses.

Pray and ask the Lord to reveal the lies you believe in this area, then confess—one at a time—the sins you have committed in this area of your life. Make sure to identify what you used to believe (the lie) but now know isn't biblical, and state the biblical truth with its godly attitudes and behaviors: "The Bible teaches that…" Depend actively upon the Holy Spirit in applying and enabling you in your commitment to know the truth and enjoy freedom to obey the Lord.

The point isn't how many verses you have memorized, but how many areas of your life have been transformed! Stop collecting verses as "trophies" when the only trophy that heaven celebrates is your life of holiness.

Renew Your Mind by Turning the Scriptures into a Prayer

This is a wonderful habit of holiness for you to use on a regular basis. Take scriptures that are particularly meaningful to you at the time and pray them back to the Lord. This is easy to do with passages taken from the Psalms, Proverbs, Ephesians, Colossians, and Philippians. As you pray these scriptures to the Lord, a different part of your life will be influenced and transformed. Usually meditation touches your mind, and prayerful meditation touches your mind and heart.

As you read and meditate on the scriptures, make sure you record personal notes and insights right in your biblical text. Write down the dates when the Lord especially communicates to you through a particular passage. One of my earliest Bible professors in Bible college showed us his Bible in class one day—it had lines and arrows and colors and circles and notes everywhere! I couldn't believe it, and wondered if I should do that to my Bible. Now, over 30 years later, I would strongly encourage you to do that very thing. Whenever I reach over to pick up my Bible, I always simultaneously pick up that blue or red pen to mark what I learn right in the text. This will help change the way you look at the Bible. The Bible is a priceless gift from the Lord for the entire body of Christ as well as for each one of us individually. The more you bring your life into the clear agenda of the Bible and use it for its intended purposes, the more you will experience the fulfillment of God's promise of your transformation into the very image of Jesus Christ:

> All Scripture is given by inspiration of God, and is profitable for doctrine, for reproof, for correction, for instruction in righteousness, that the man of God may be complete, thoroughly equipped for every good work (2 Timothy 3:16-17).

OTHER GOOD HARVEST HOUSE READING FROM BRUCE WILKINSON

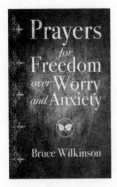

Prayers for Freedom over Worry and Anxiety

No matter what's making you anxious, God cares!

Set your heart free as you are encouraged by God's truth and empowered by His love. Be uplifted as you read short devotions to quiet your mind, scripture to guide your thoughts, and prayers to help you convey your burdens to the Lord, who can handle them all. Burdens such as...

- staying safe
- navigating your finances
- repairing relationships
- maintaining good health
- facing the future

Are you ready to release your worries and receive God's infinite peace? This book will help you in your daily prayer time, enhancing your current experience and freeing you to fully embrace heavenly peace.

Prayers of Blessing Over Your Husband (with Heather Hair)

Are you unsure of how to best pray for your husband? Do you struggle to find words that are meaningful and honest?

Prayer is one of the most beautiful gifts you can give to your spouse, but trying to know his heart and pray with intention can feel overwhelming. You can't understand his every spiritual need—but God knows.

This book of insightful, guided prayers and carefully matched scriptures will enable you to pray for your husband with resolve and passion. Each day, your confidence will grow as you are inspired to approach God with a sincere and courageous heart for your spouse.

You can become a powerful force of prayer for your husband's life. Move from uncertainty to assurance as you devote yourself daily to conversation with the Lord who created, knows, and fiercely loves your husband.

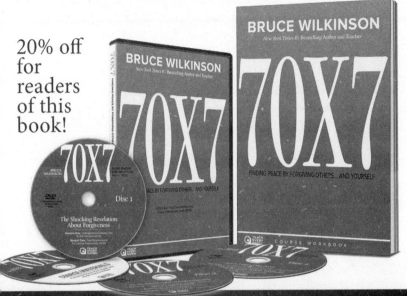
cr152

WANT A TASTE OF WHAT IT MEANS TO DREAM AGAIN?

Join Bruce Wilkinson for this life-changing 12-week course and learn the strategies to re-engage with your passions and truly live your dream.

Unlock your dream through exclusive access to this online, self-paced course offering:

· Brand NEW weekly video lessons from Bruce
· Course content
· Personal study & reflection
· A pathway to pursue your dreams!

Discover the future you've only dreamed of before!

DREAM AGAIN

12-WEEK COURSE

BRUCE WILKINSON

BruceWilkinson.com

To learn more about Harvest House books and
to read sample chapters, visit our website:

www.harvesthousepublishers.com

HARVEST HOUSE PUBLISHERS
EUGENE, OREGON